Merry
CHRISTMAS

This Books Belongs To

....

....

....

....

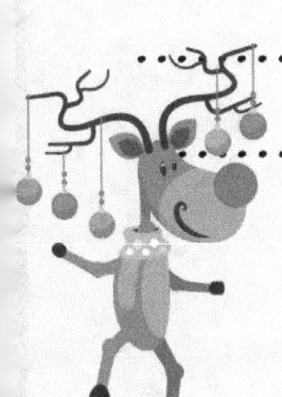
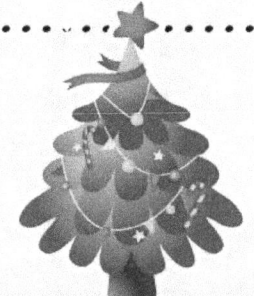
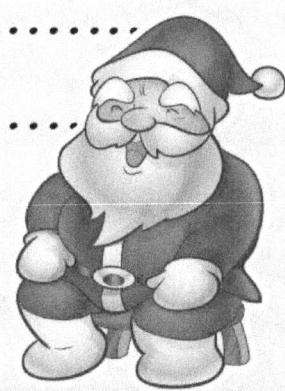

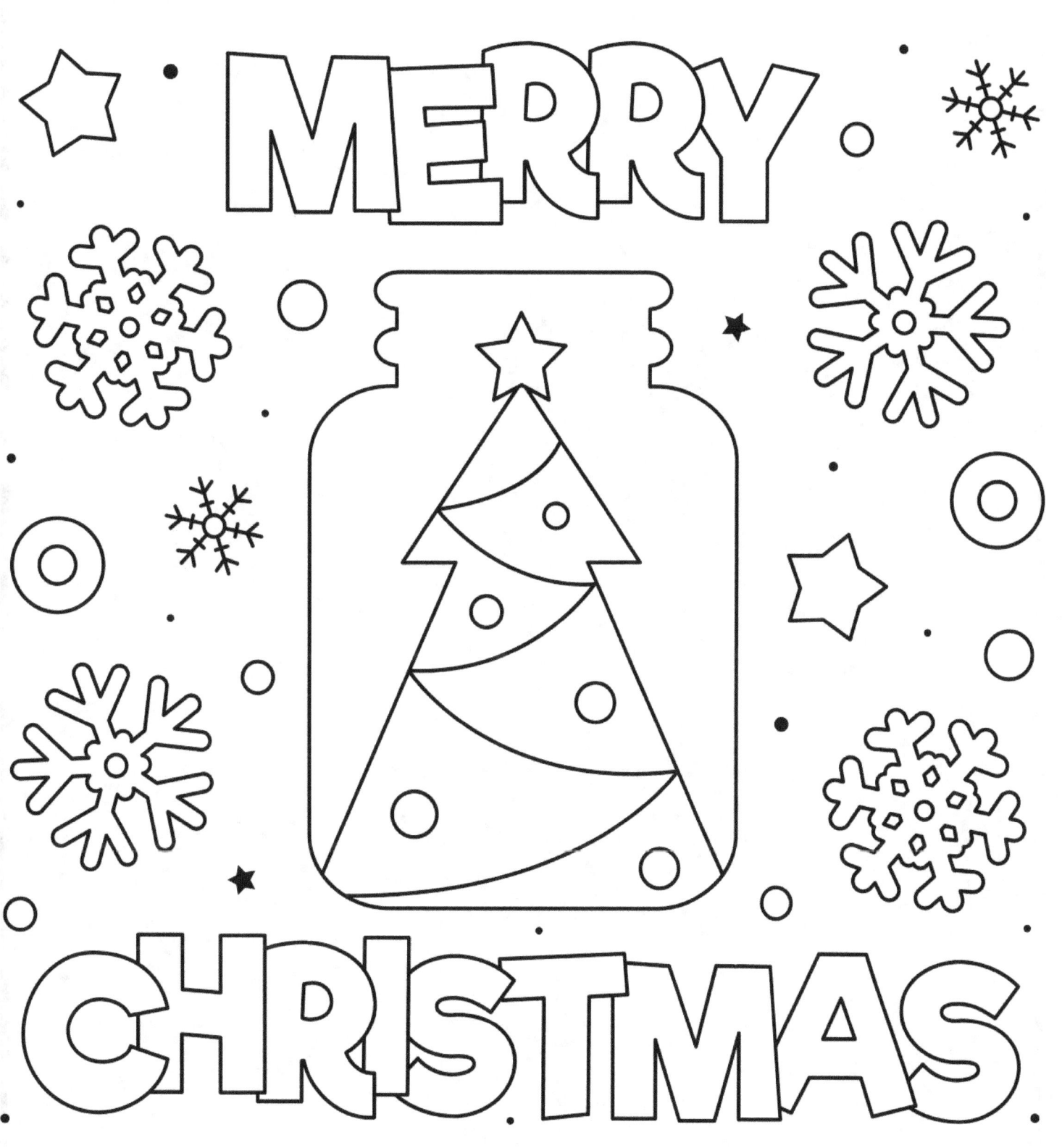

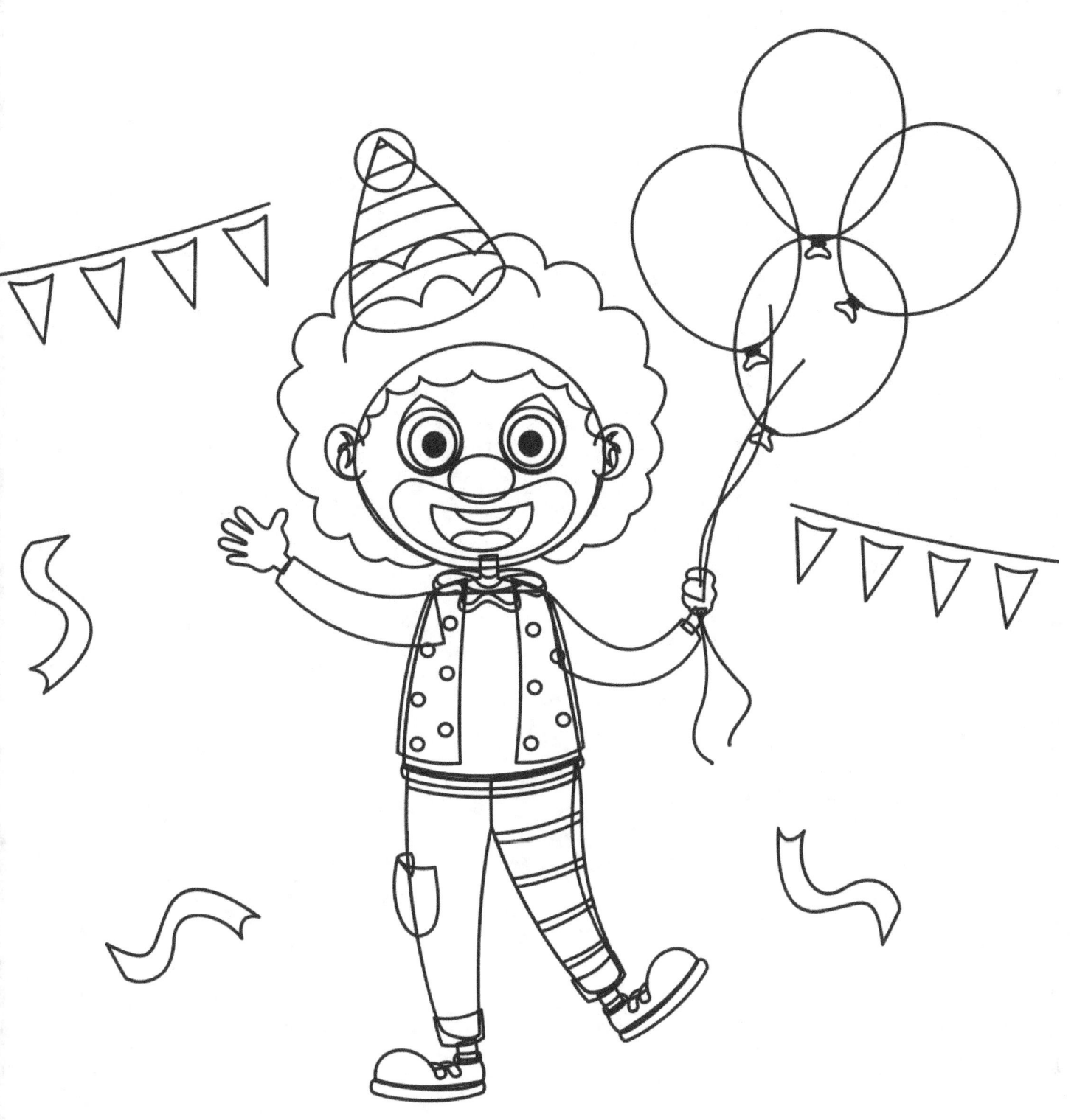

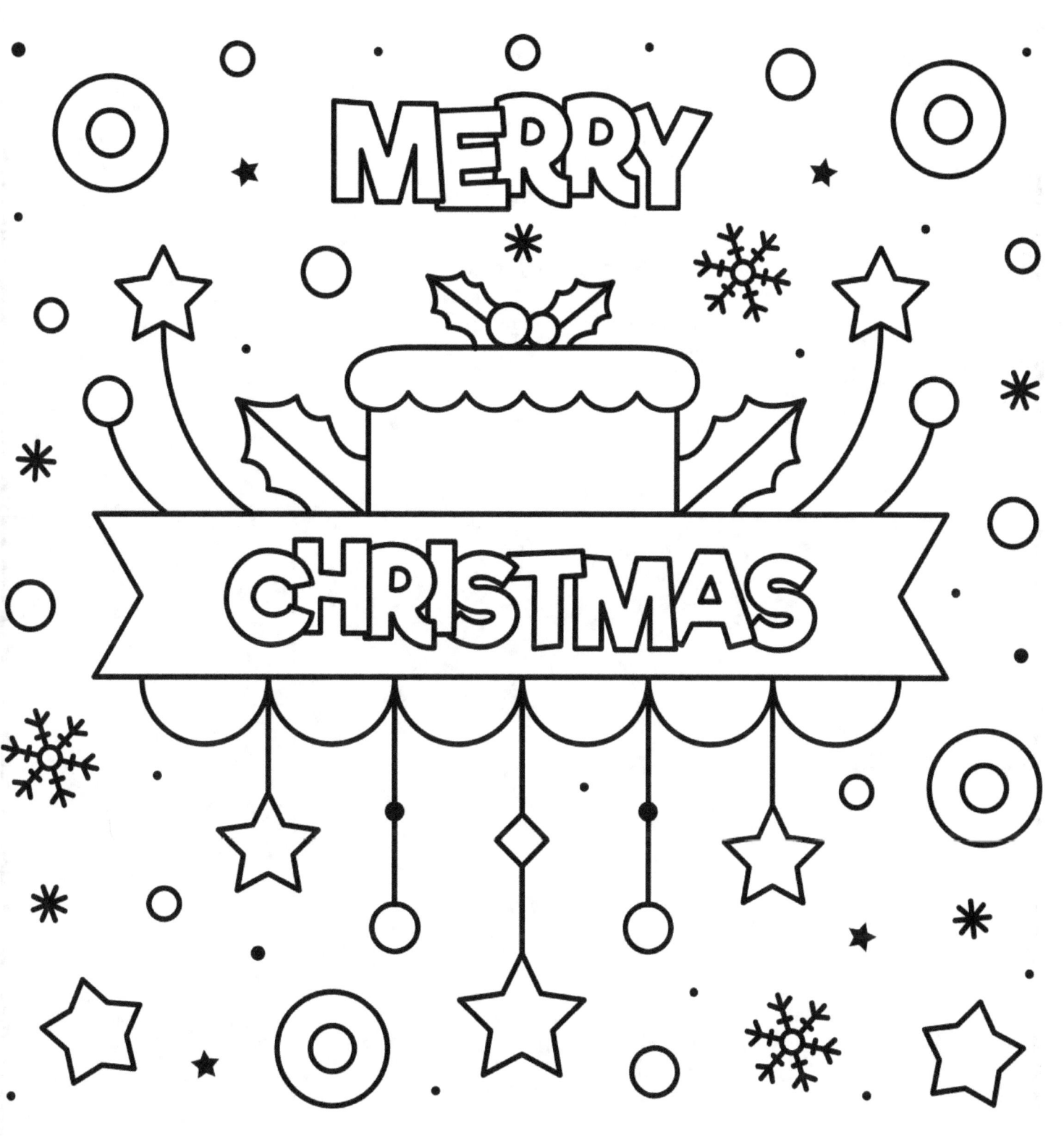

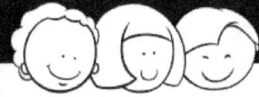

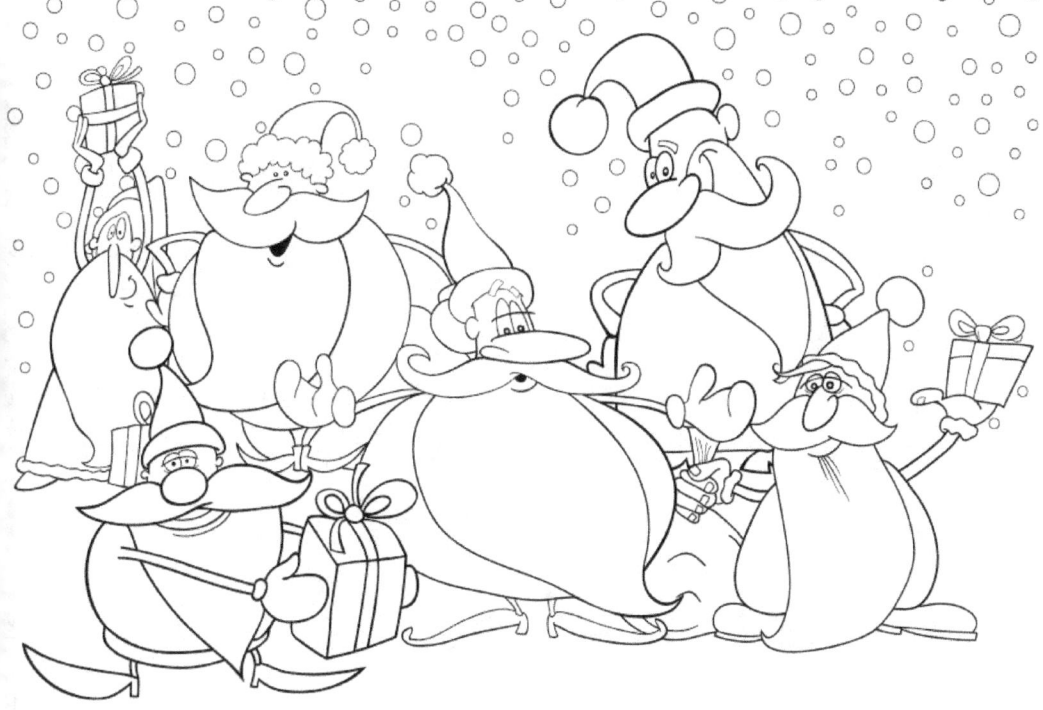

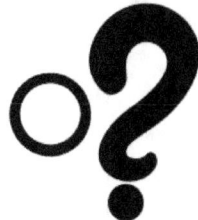

FIND
7
DIFFERENCES

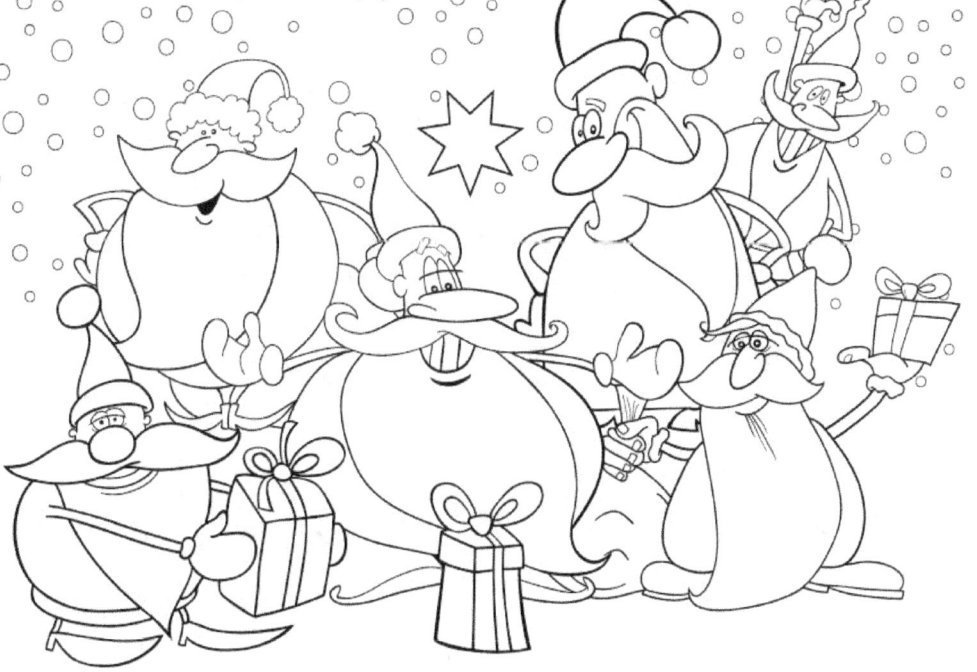

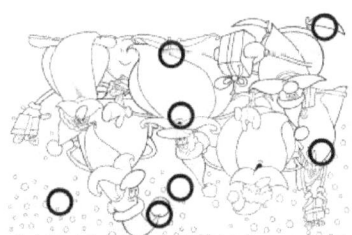

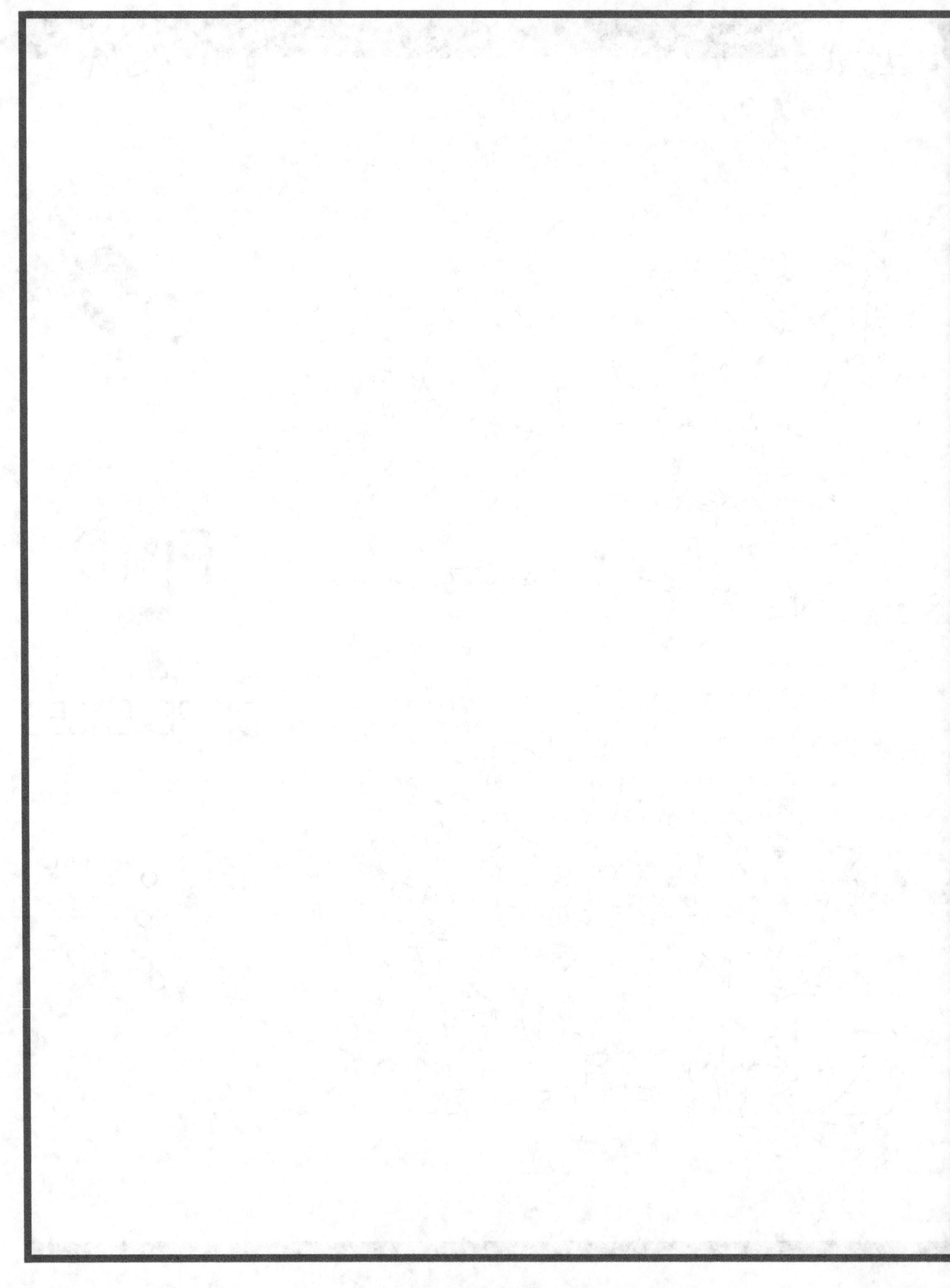

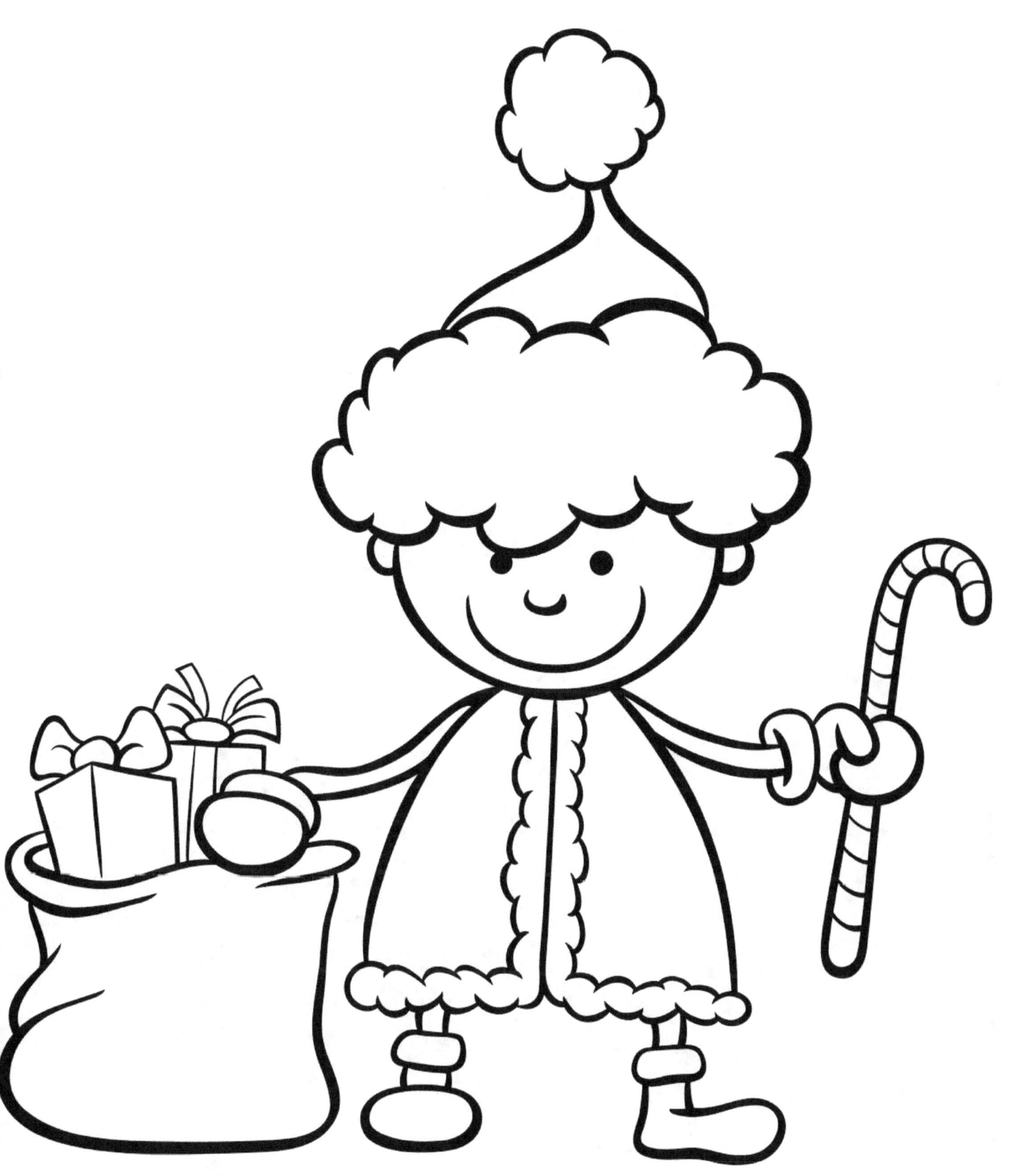

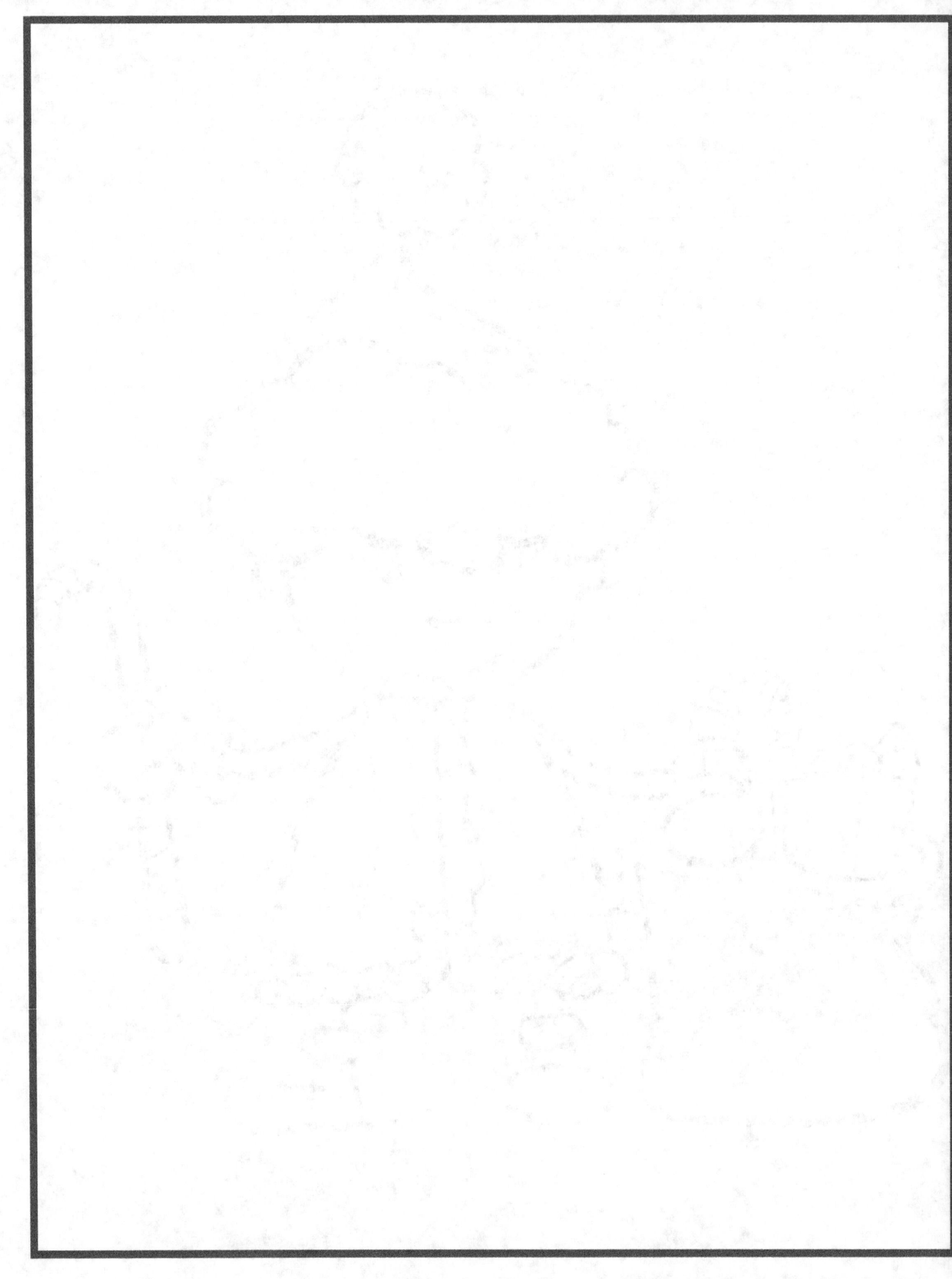

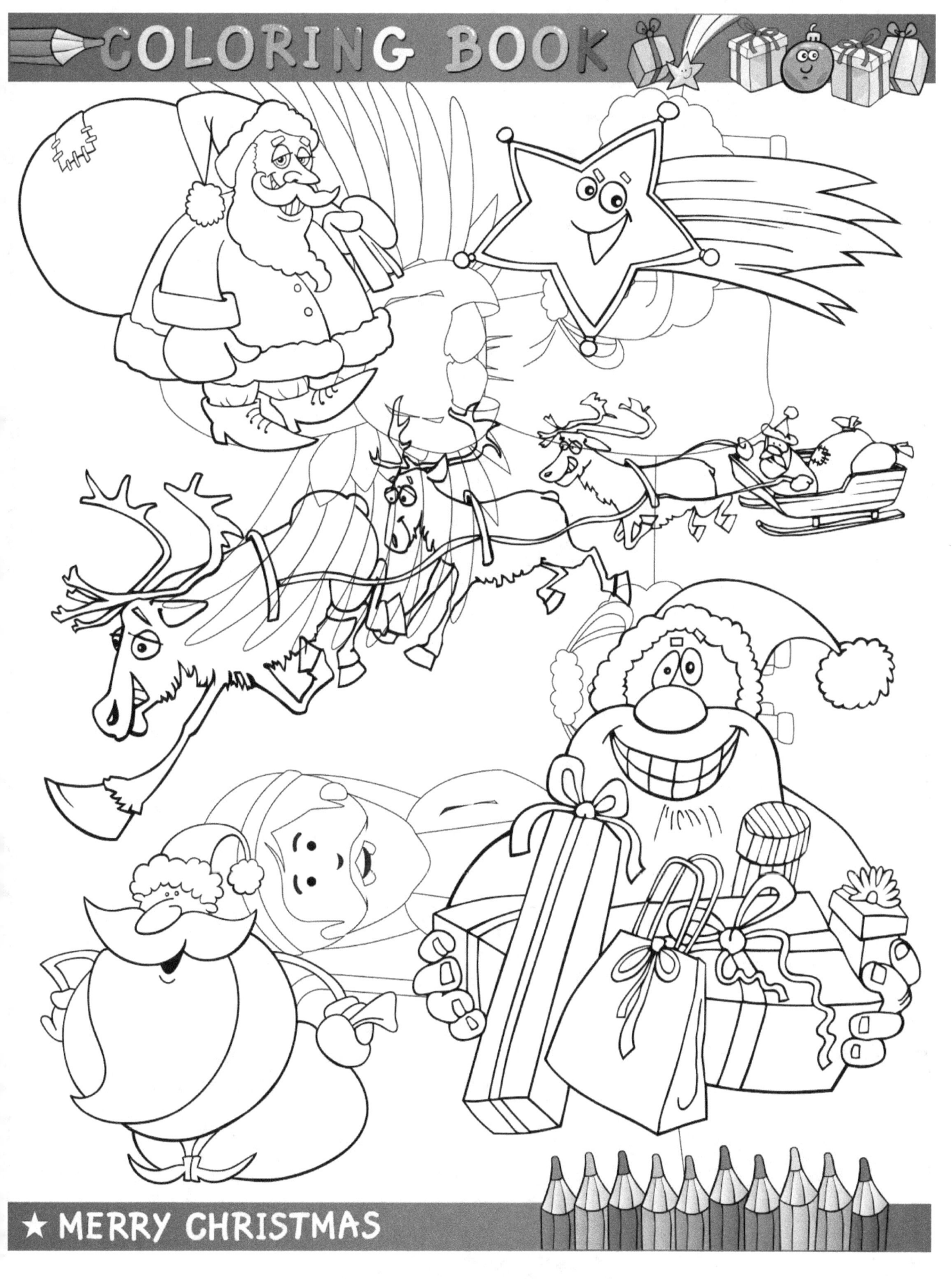

COLORING BOOK

★ MERRY CHRISTMAS

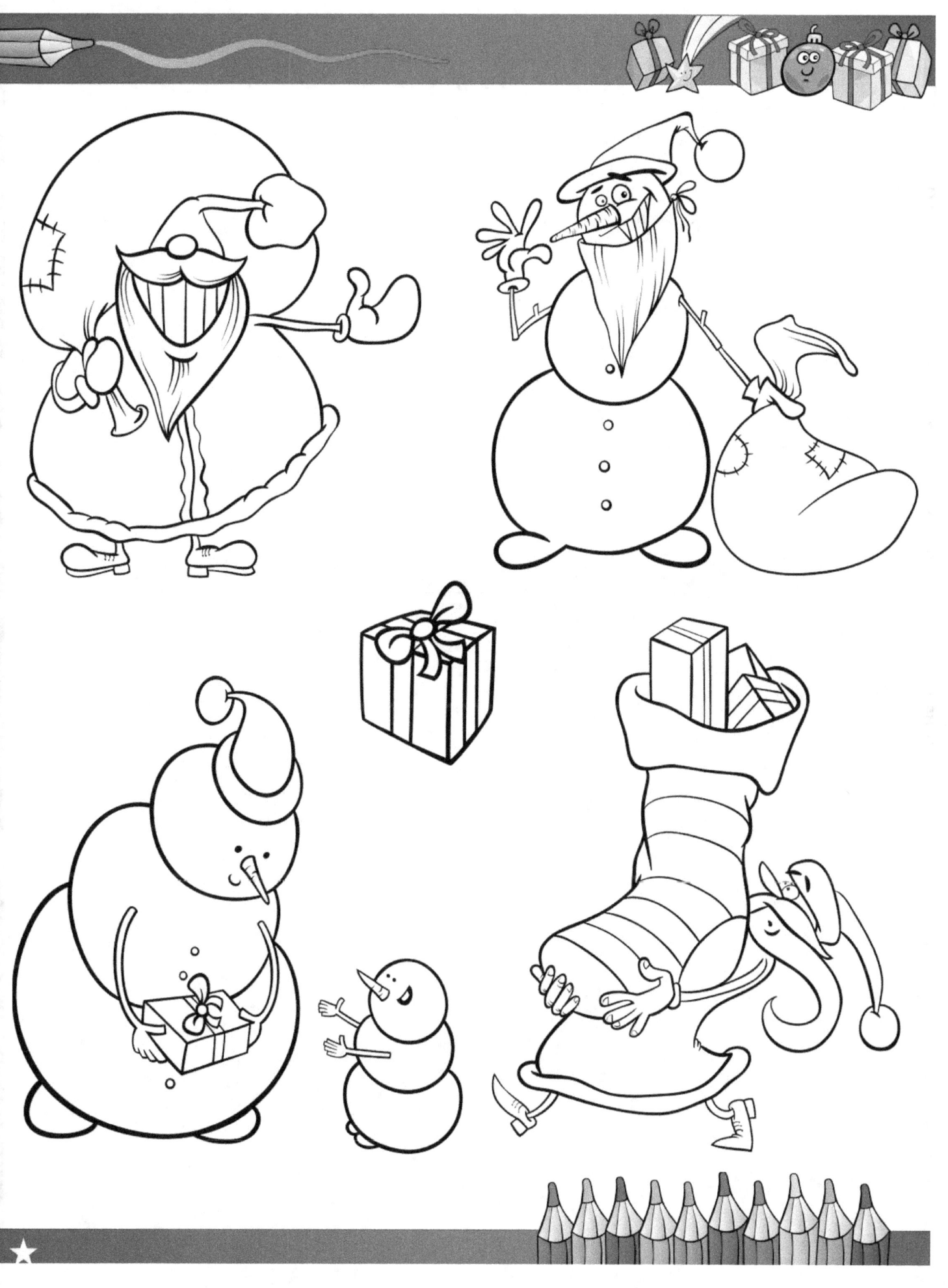

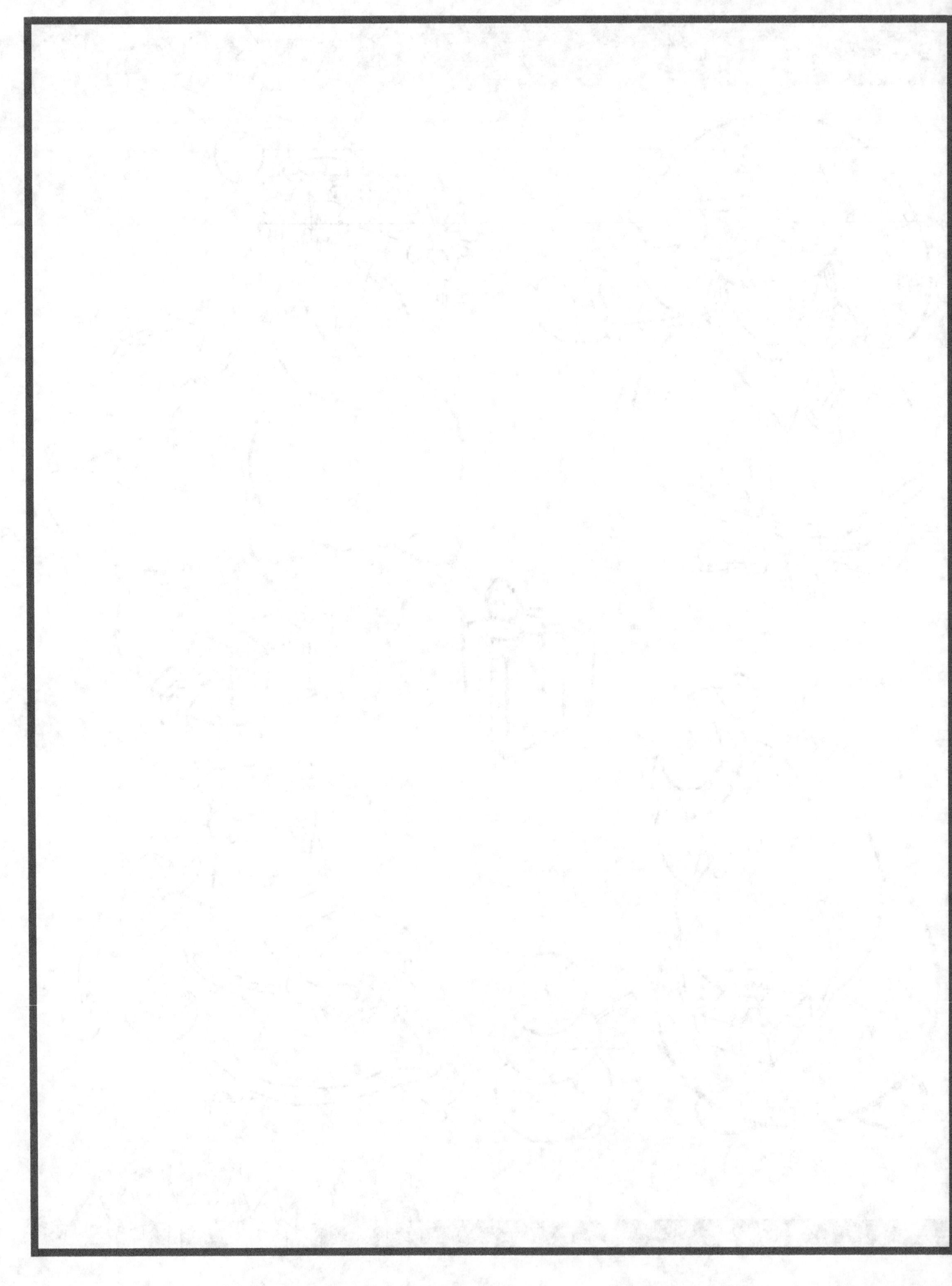

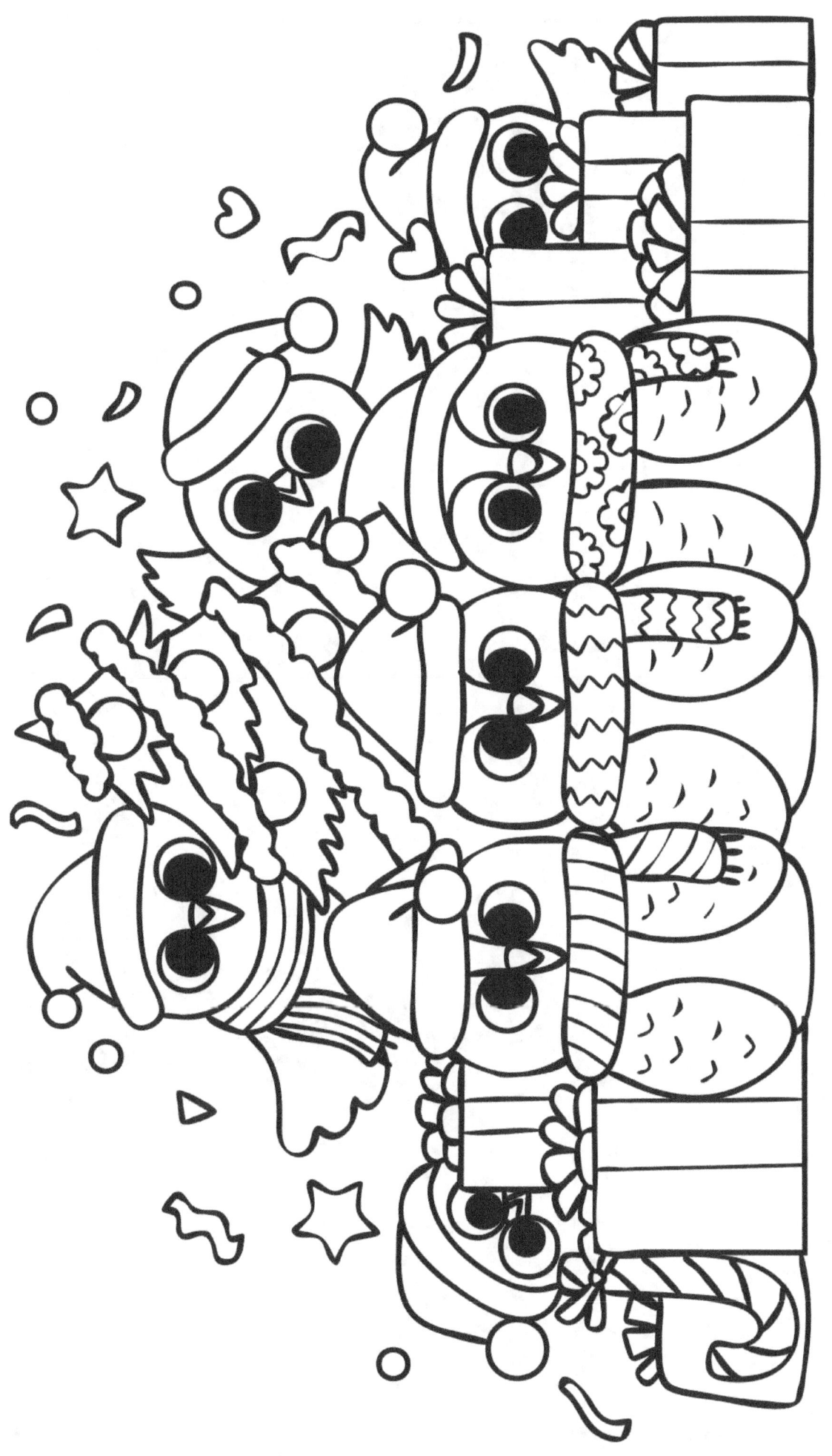

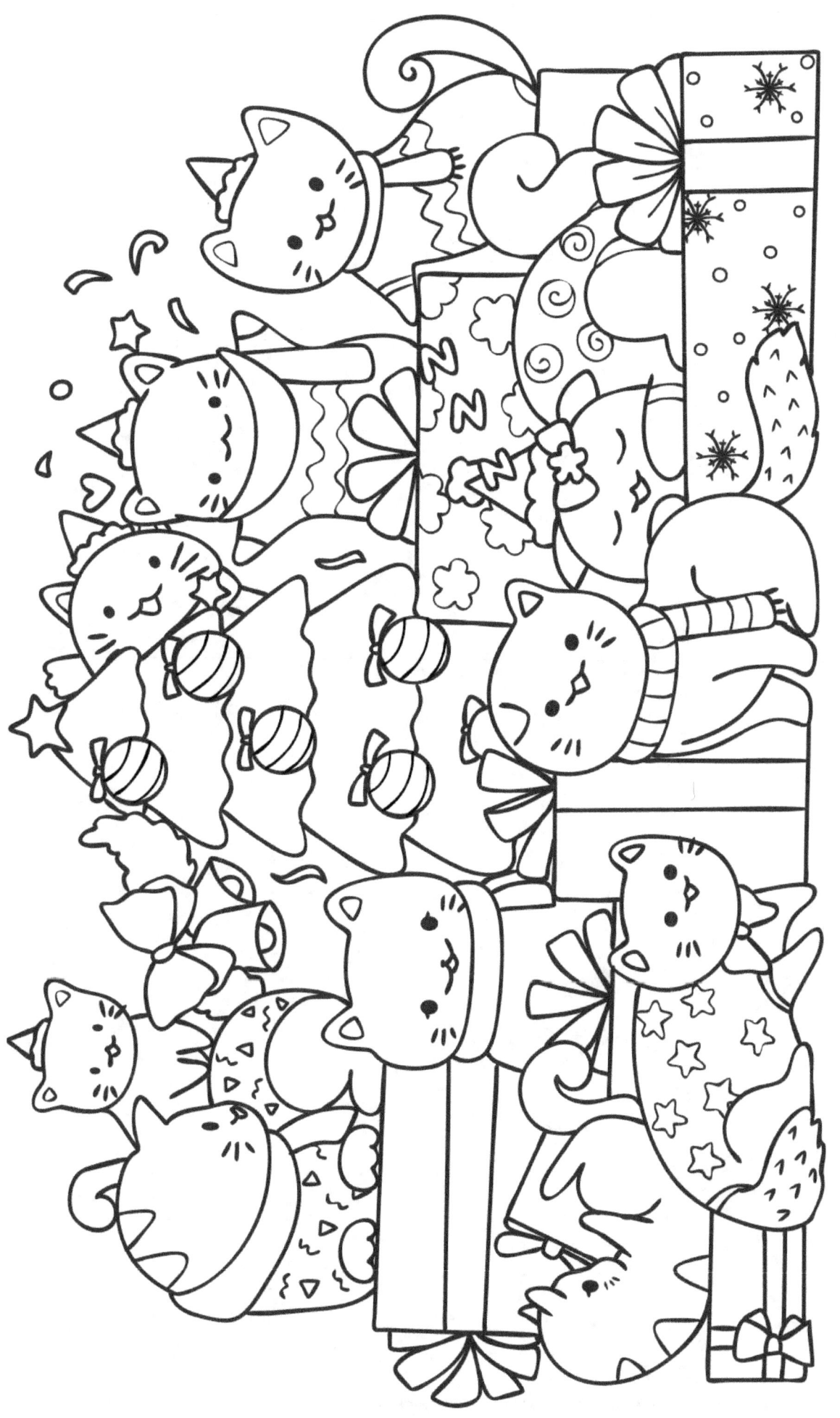

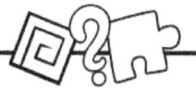

CHRISTMAS
FIND
ONE
OF A KIND

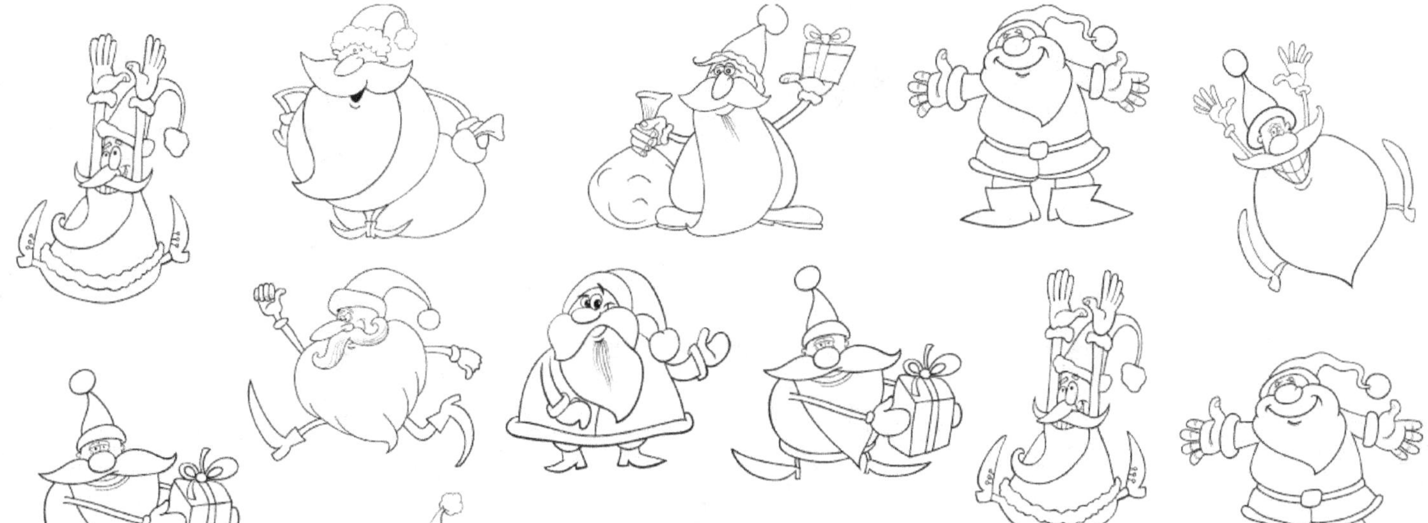

ANSWER

?

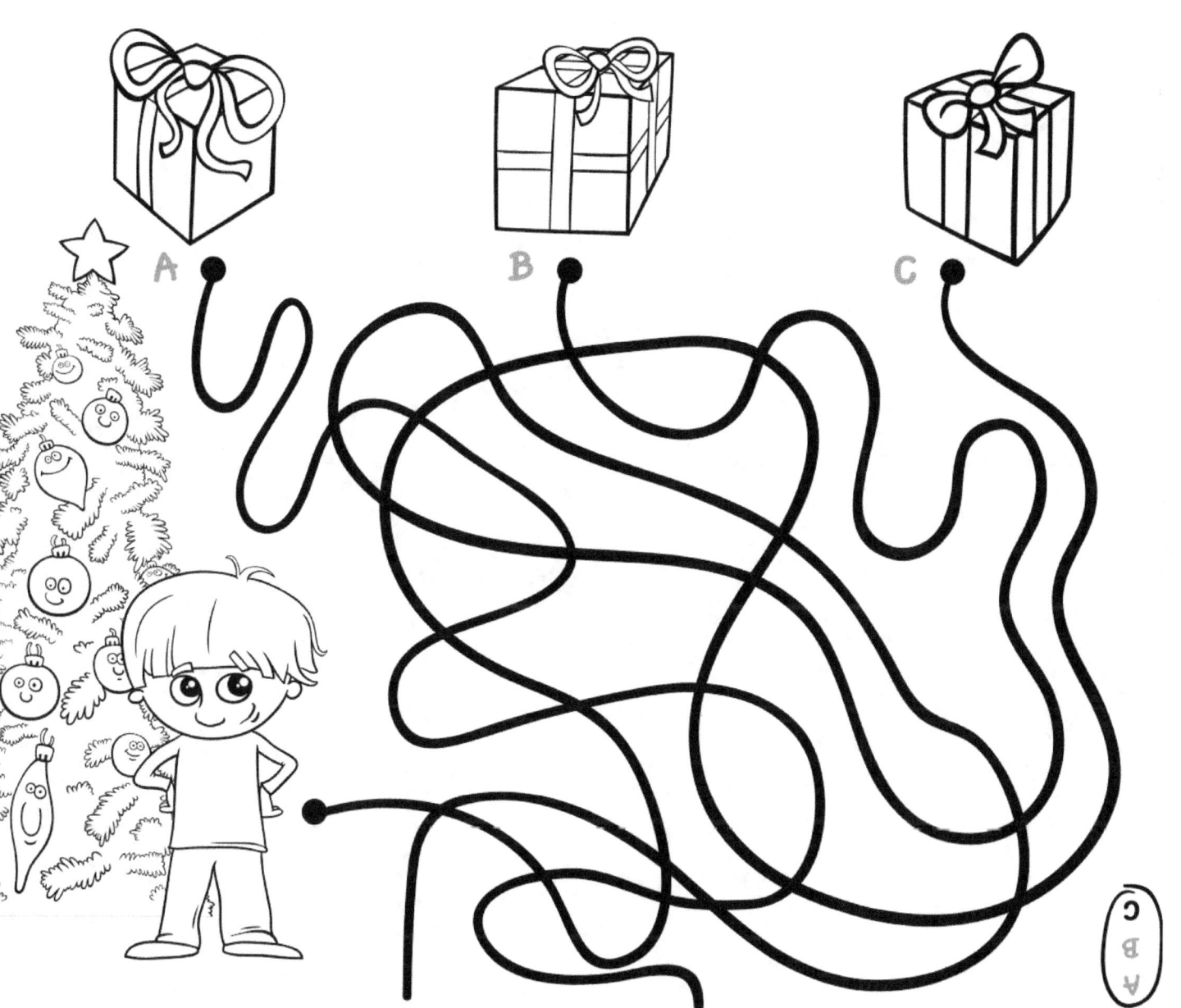

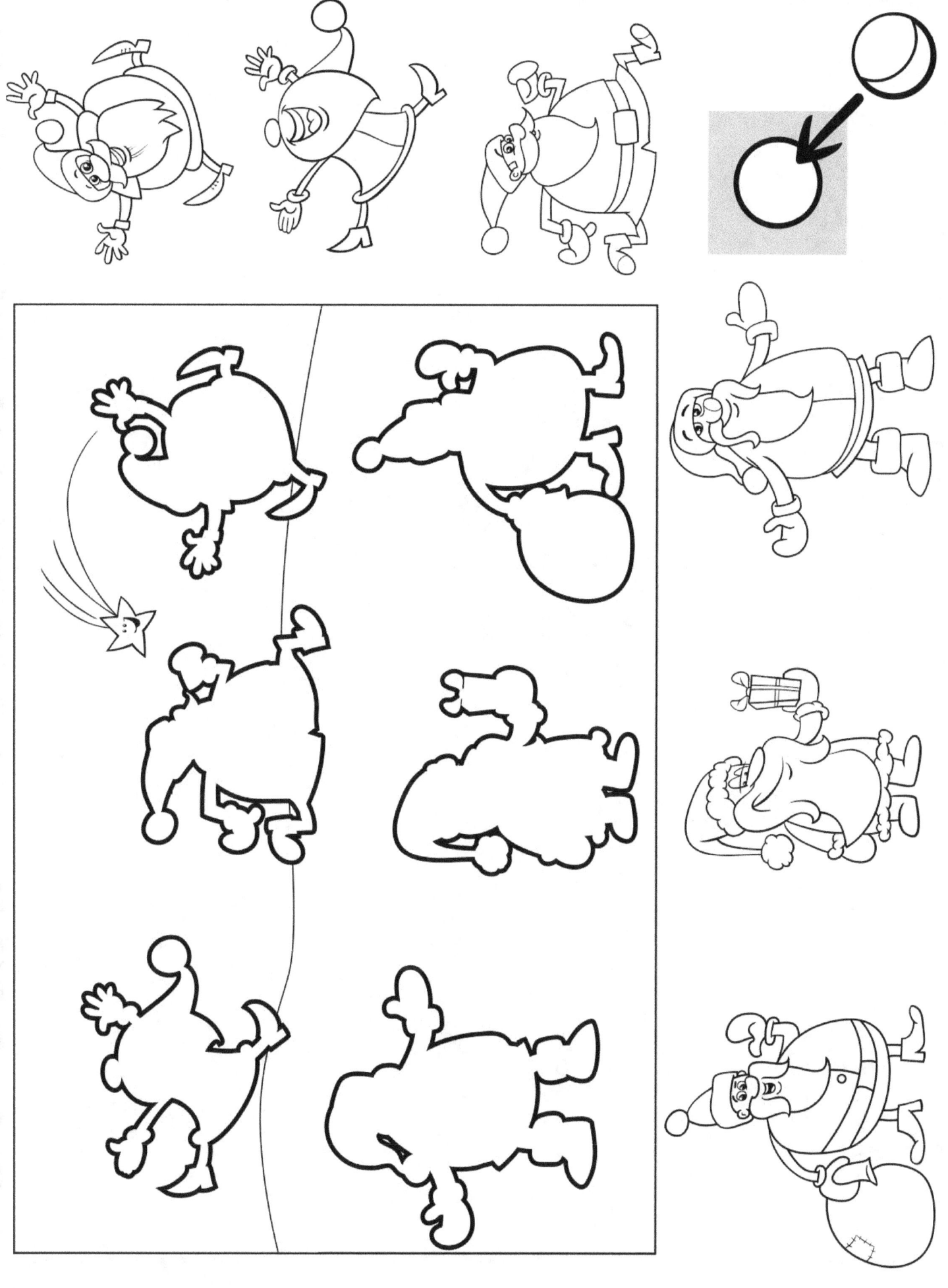

WHAT COMES NEXT?

1
2
3
4

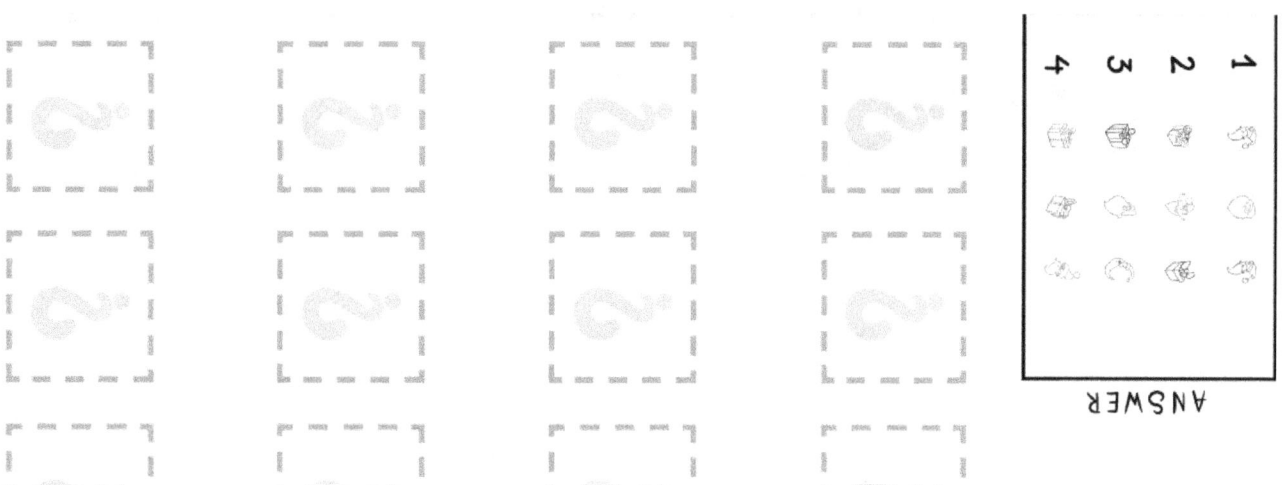

ANSWER

1
2
3
4

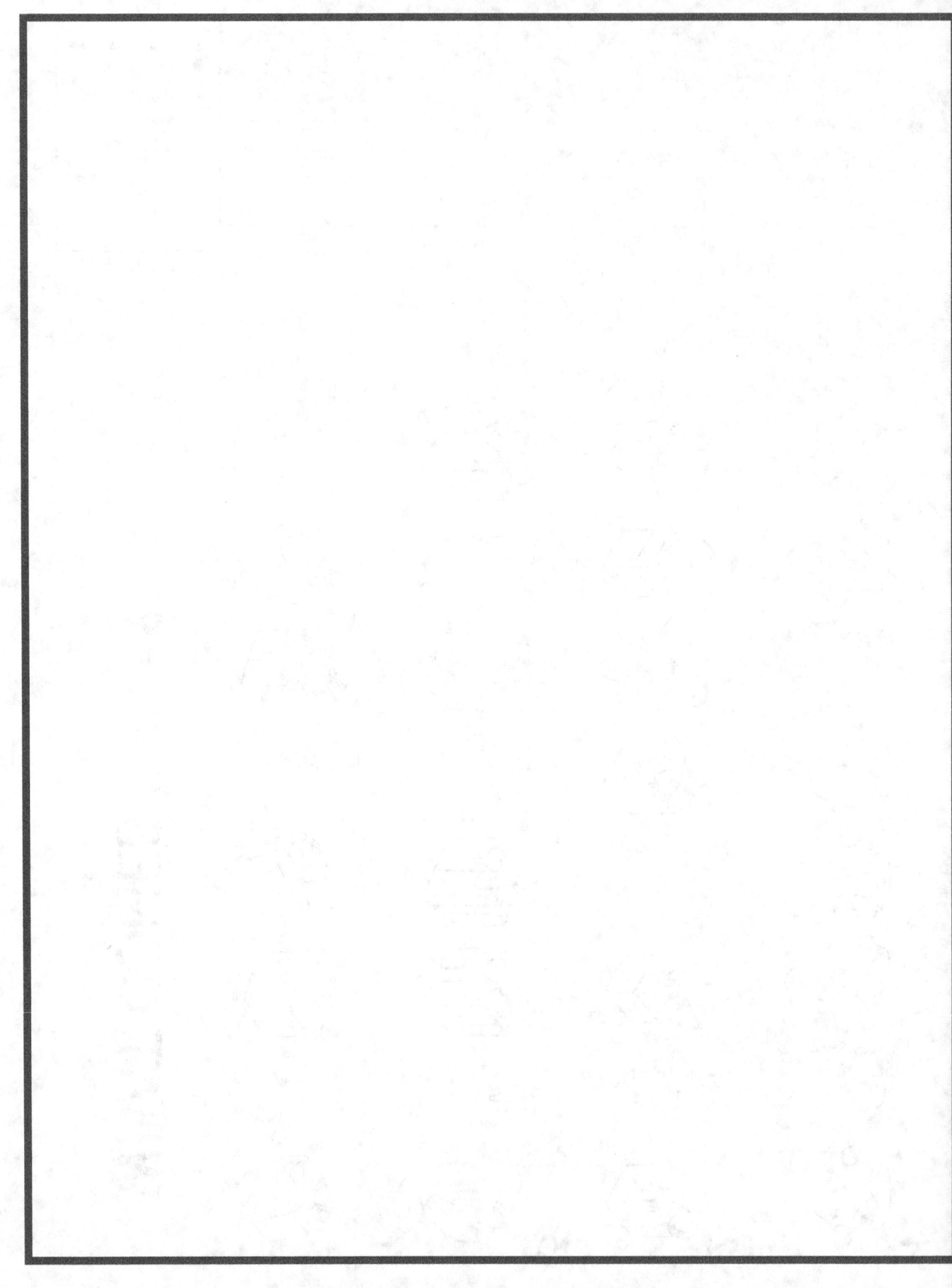

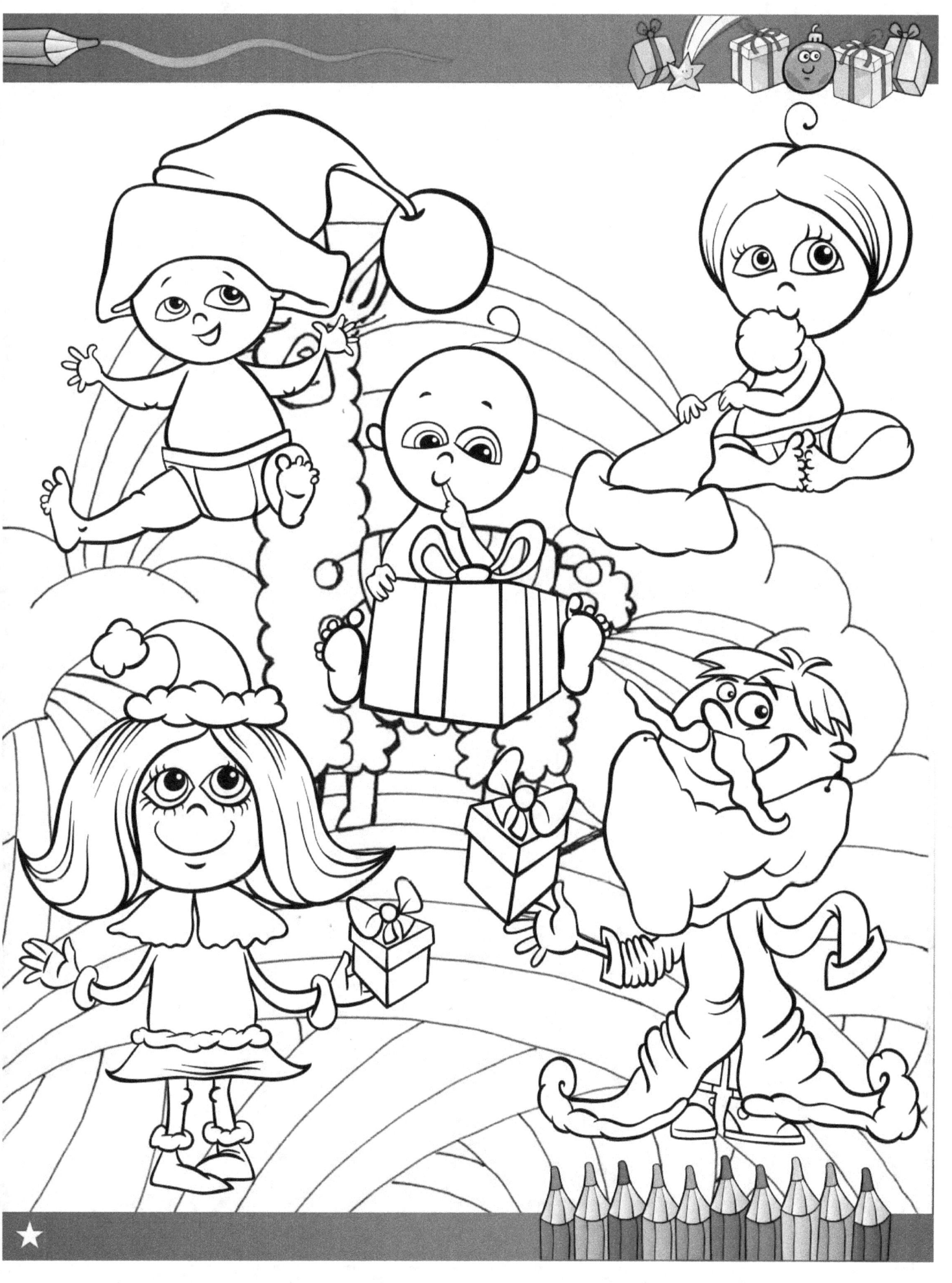

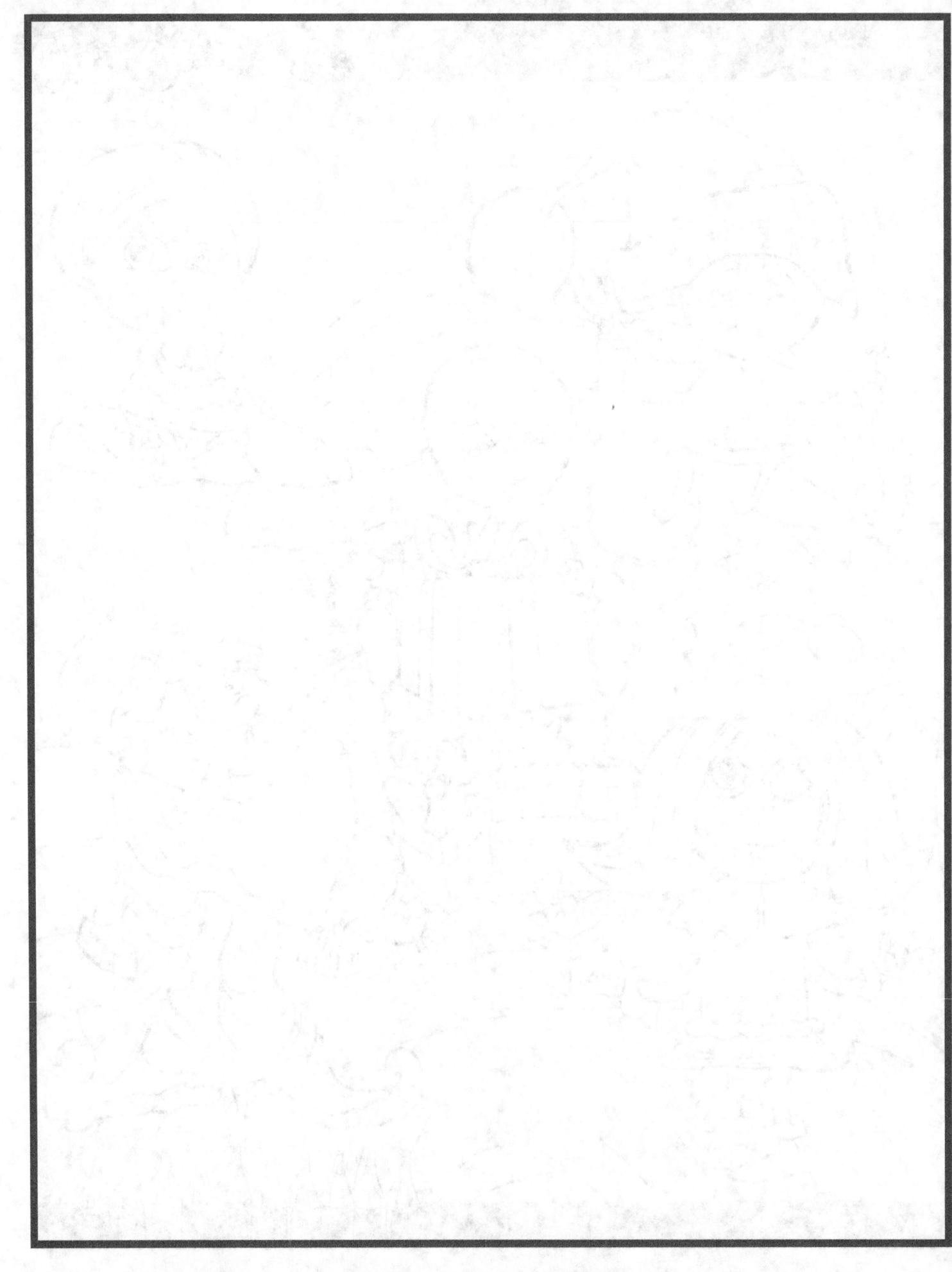

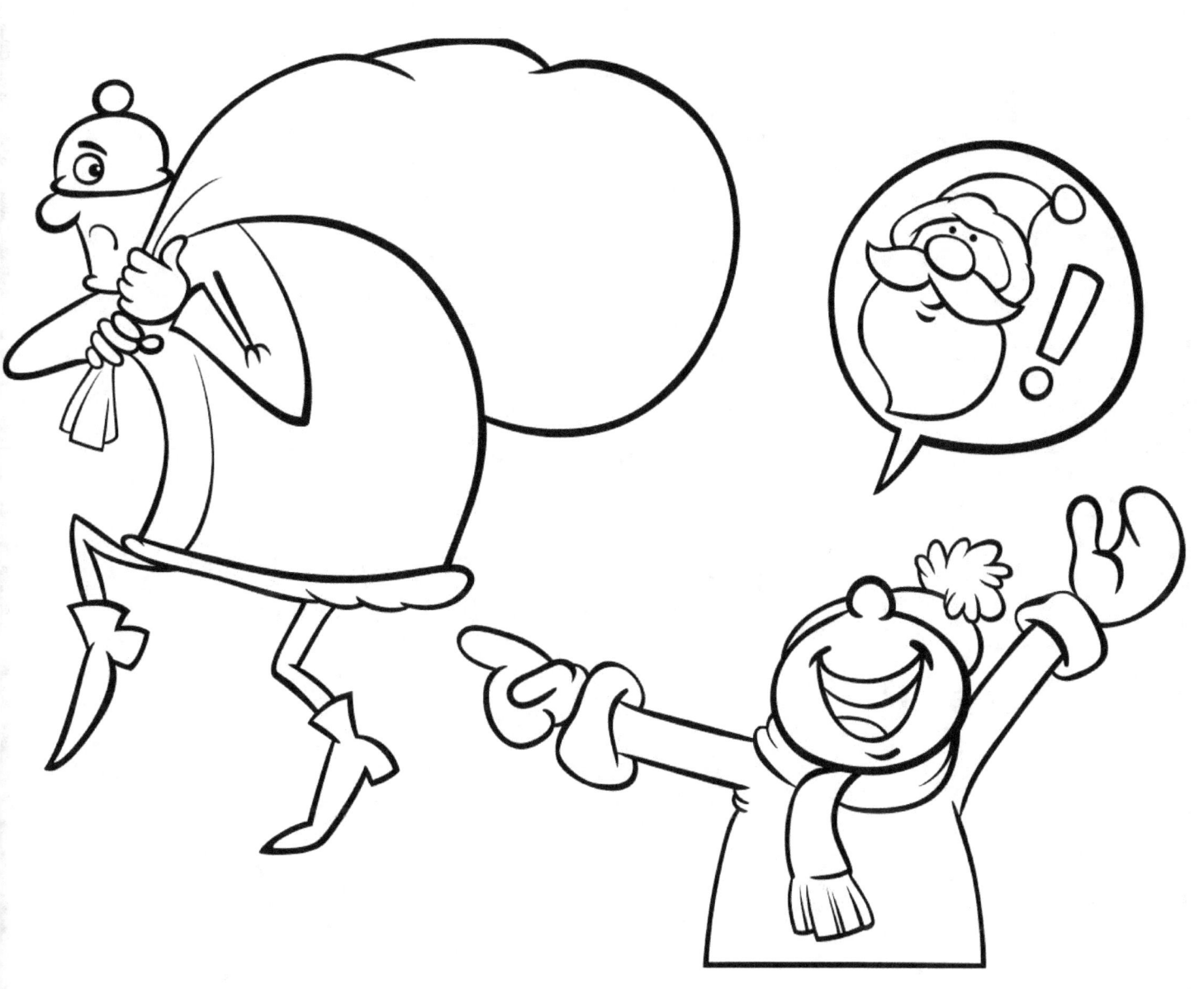

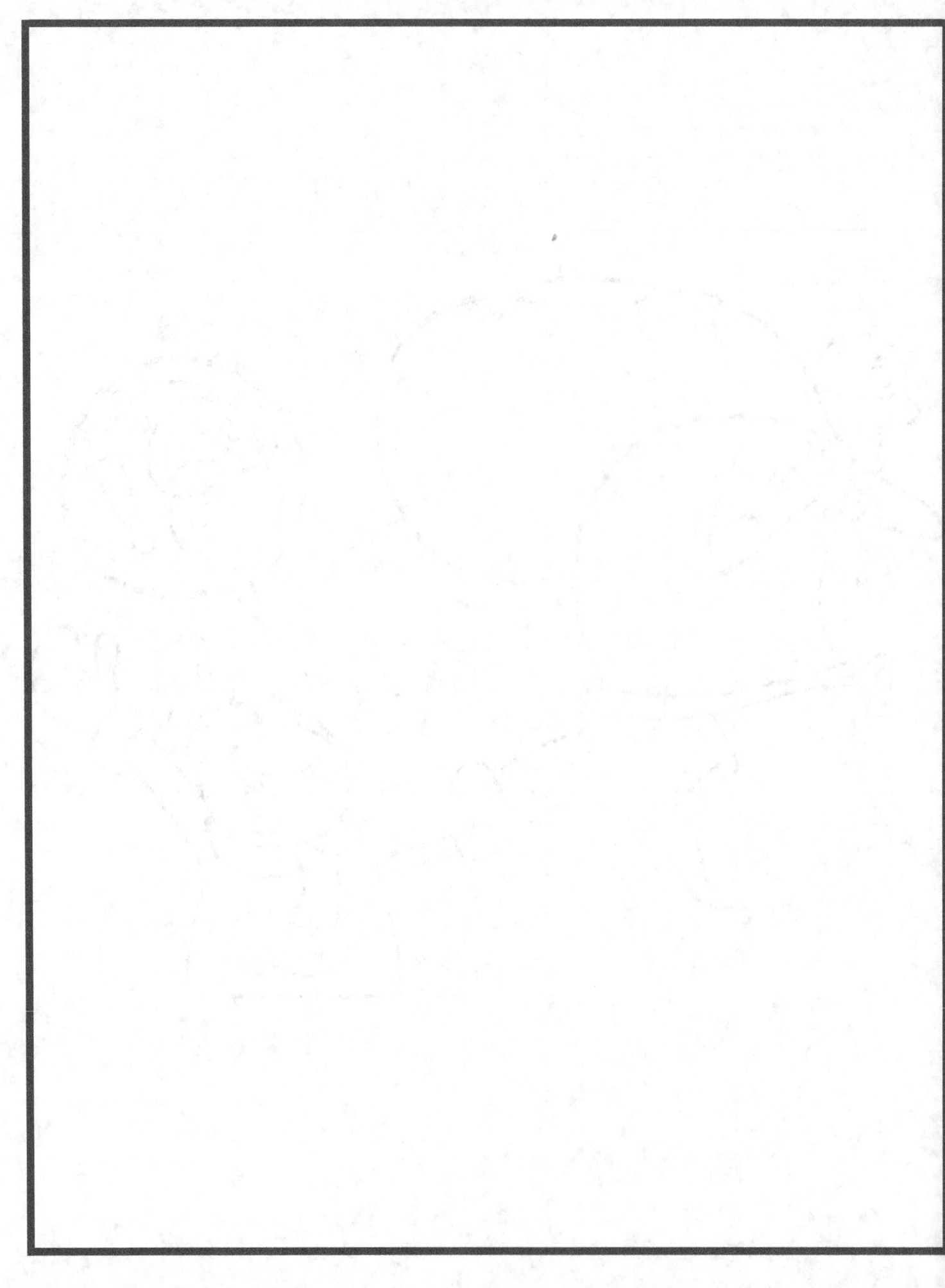

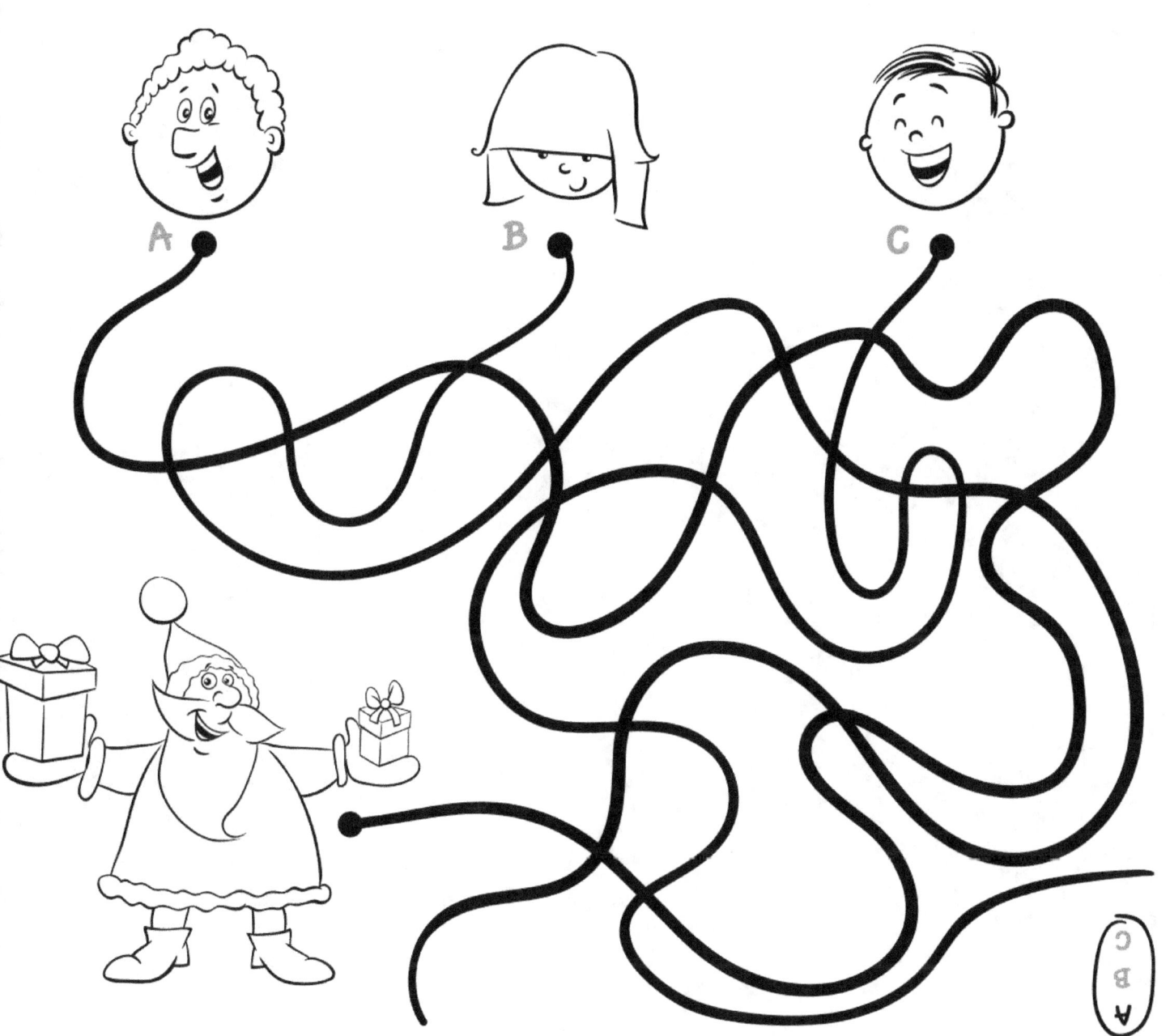

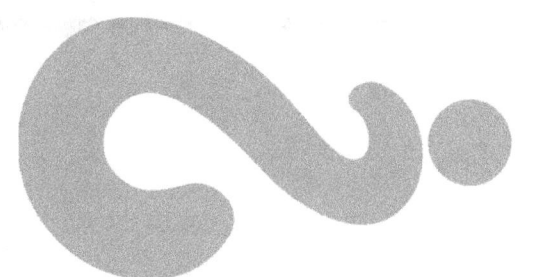

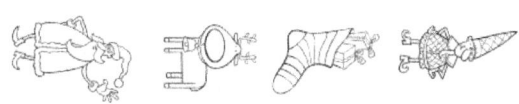

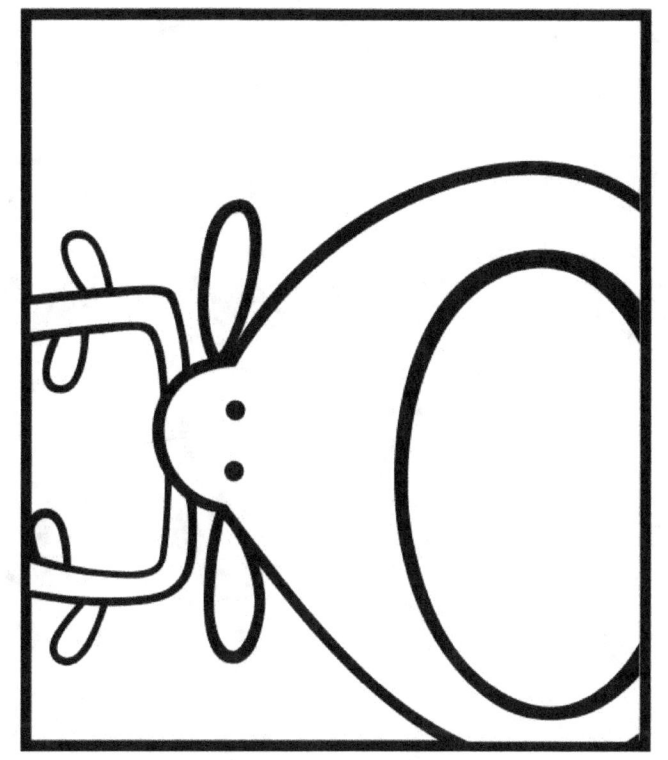

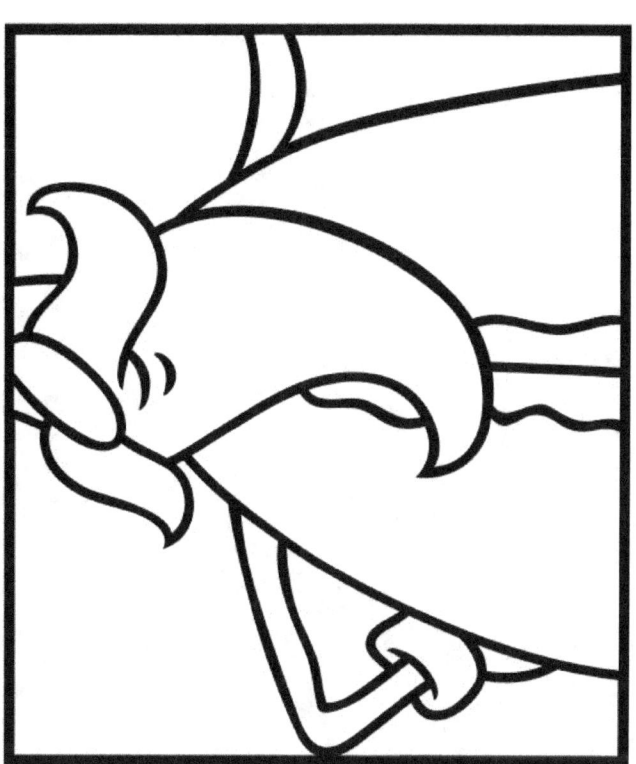

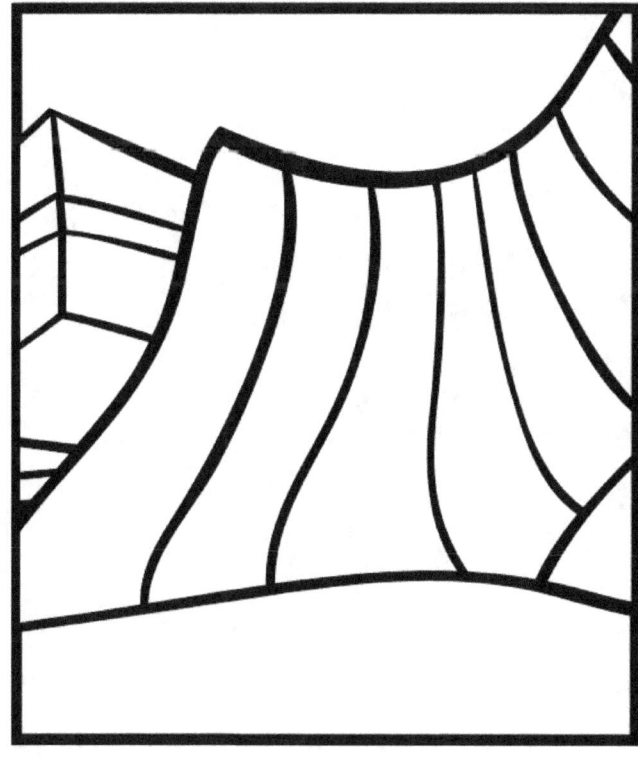

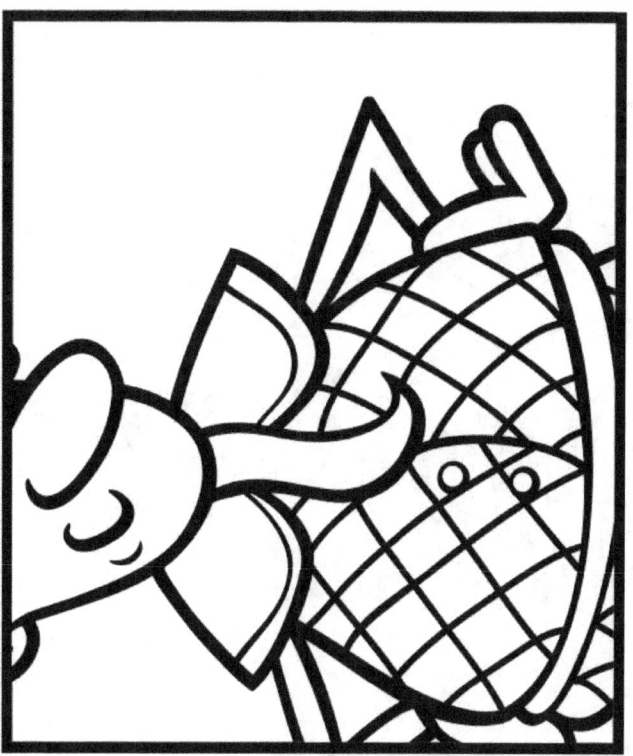

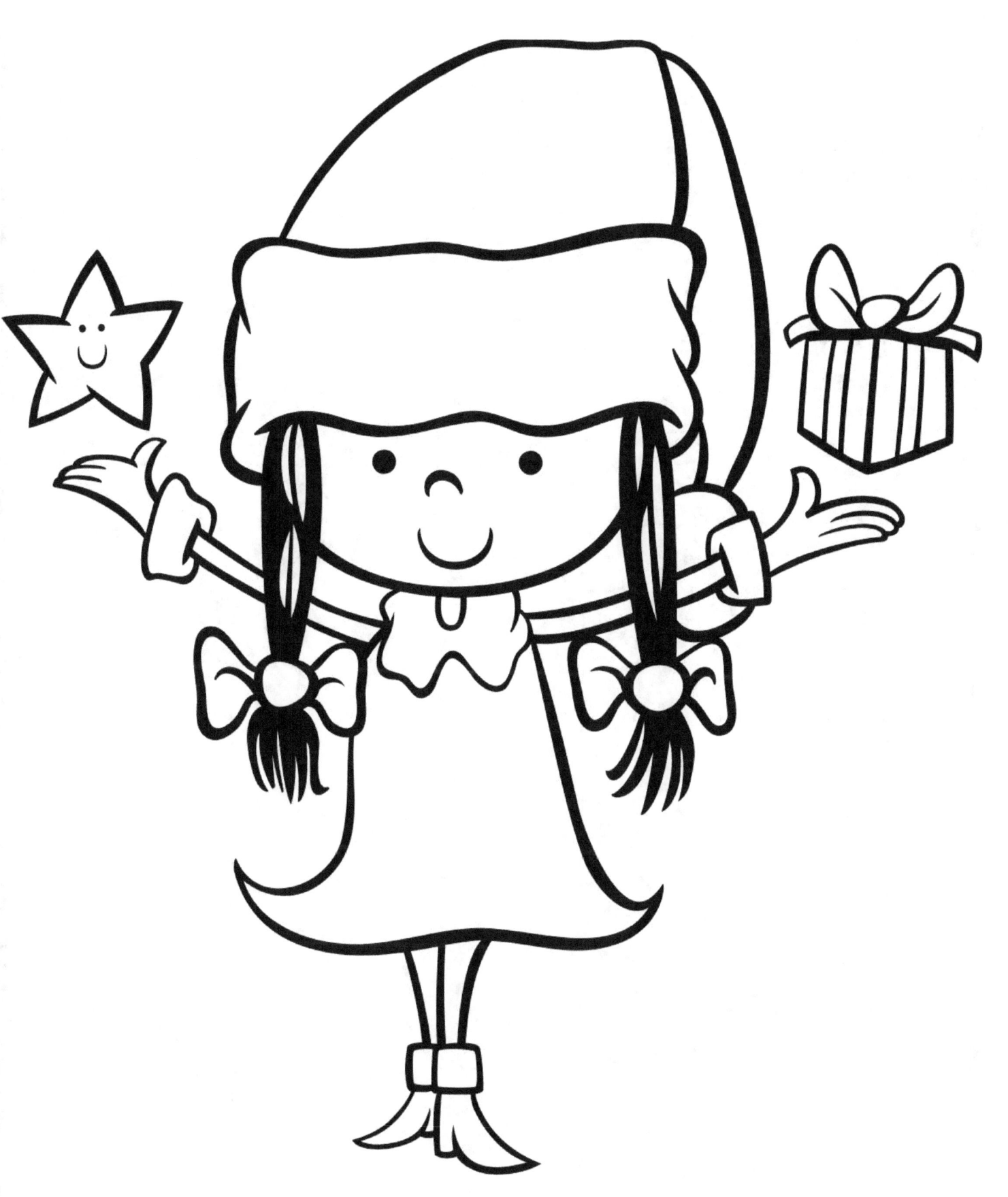

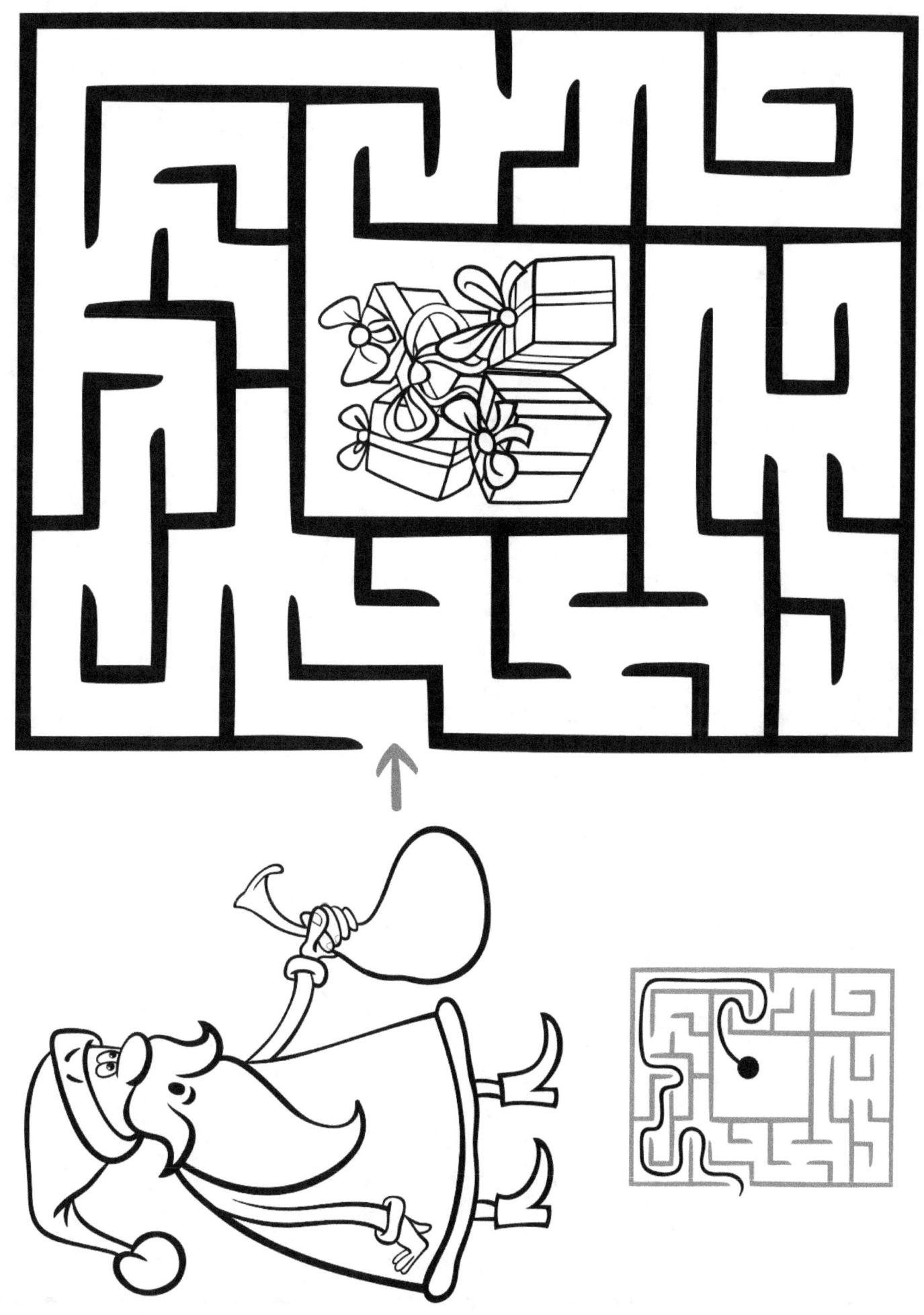

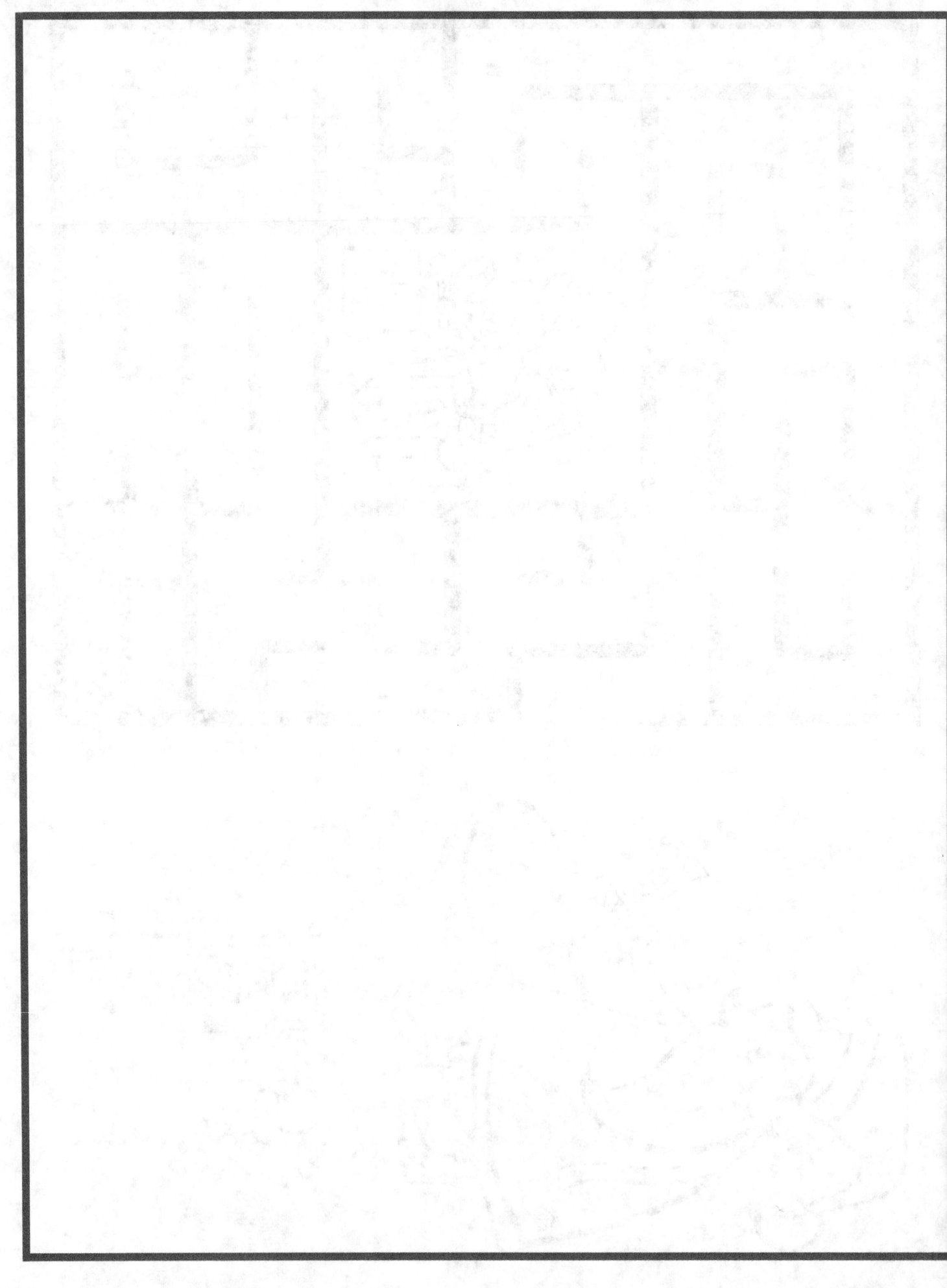

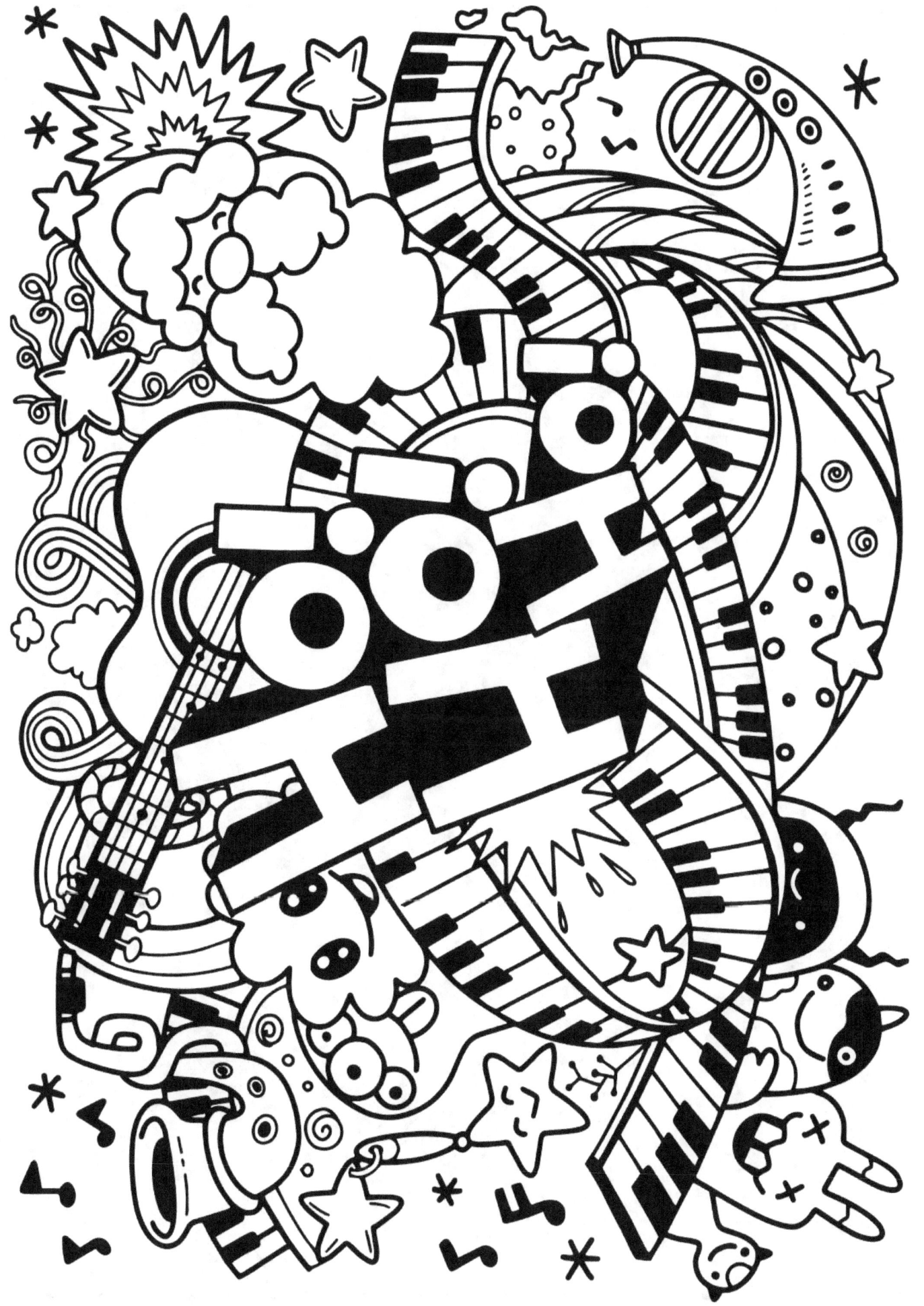

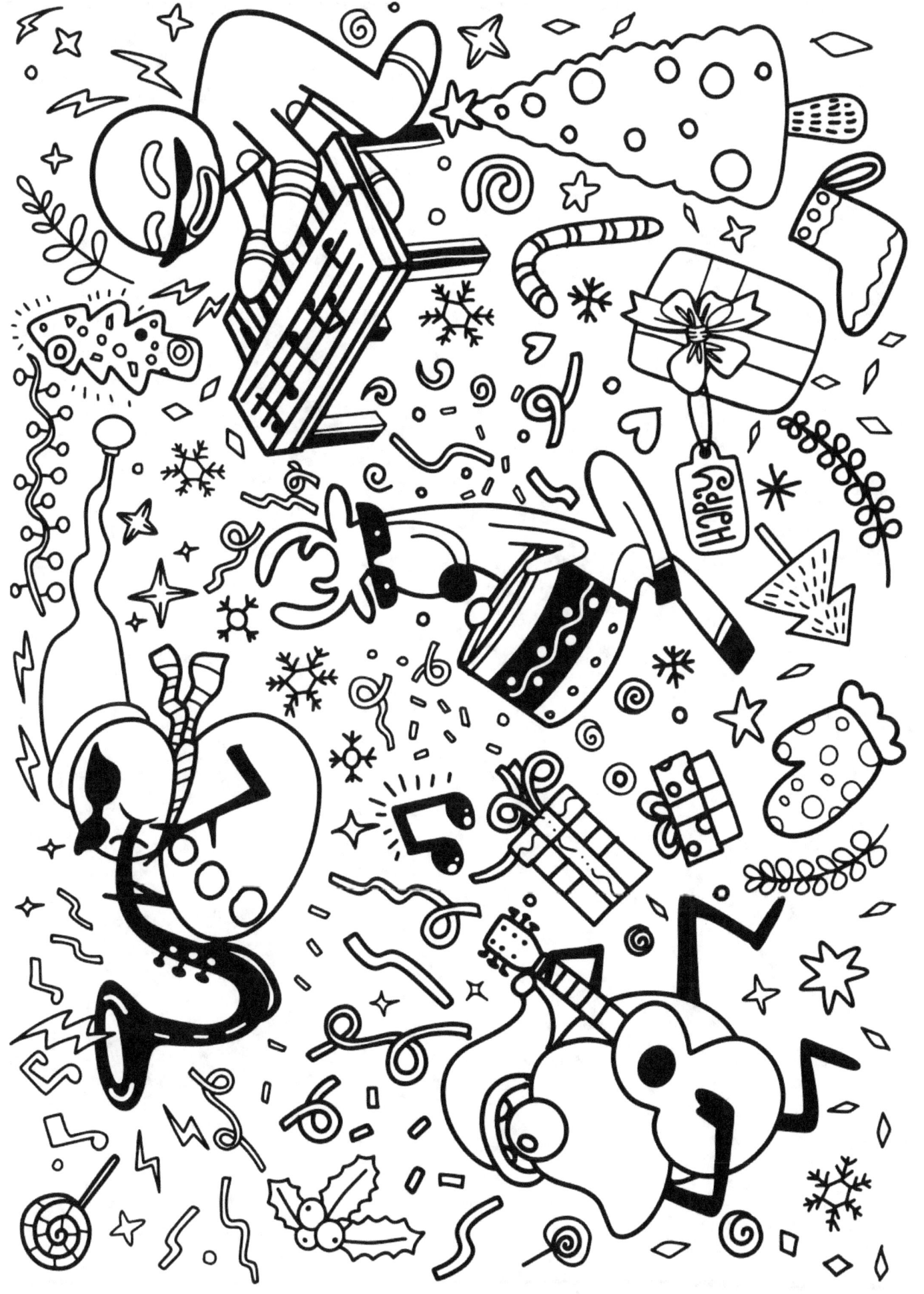

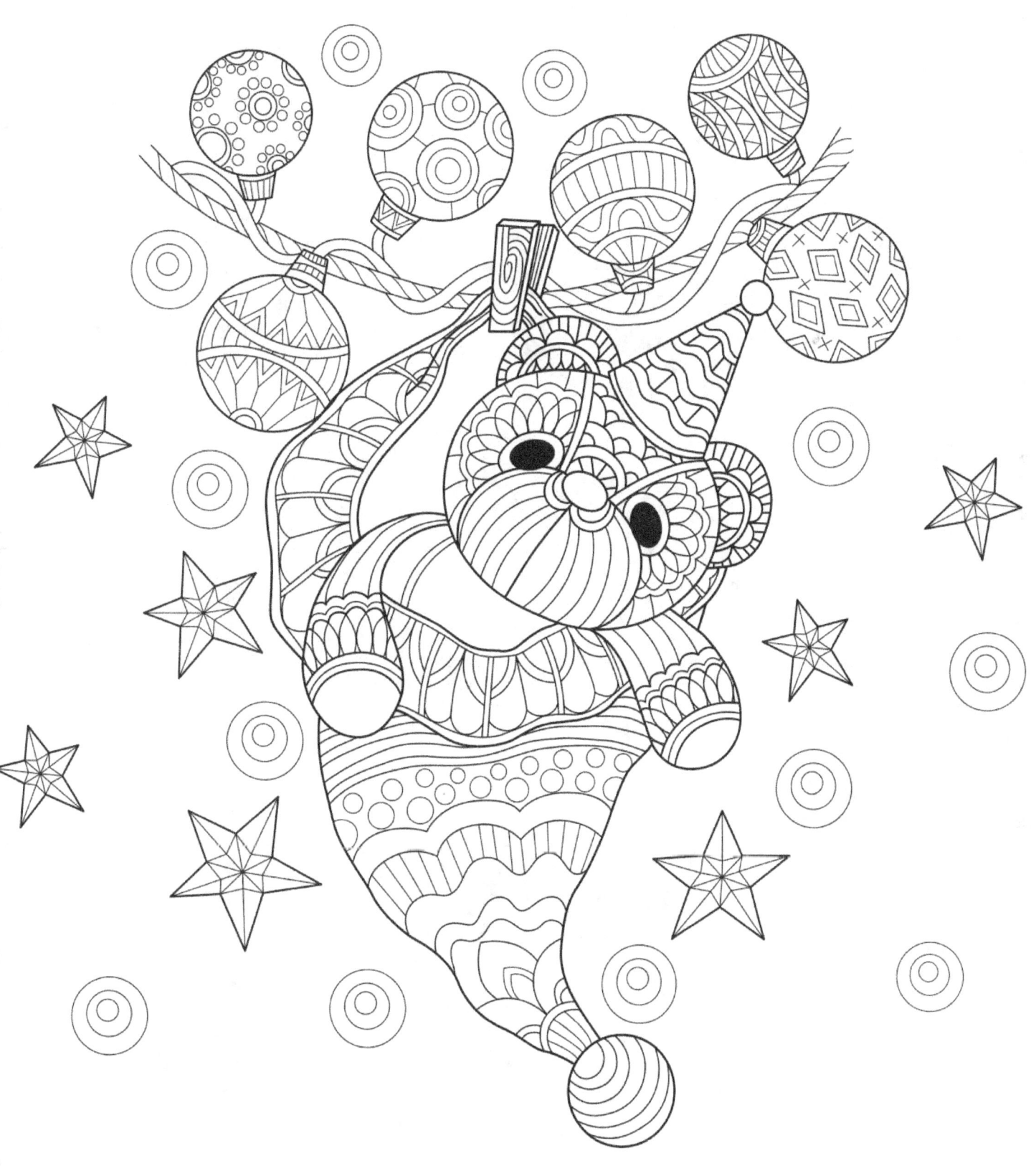

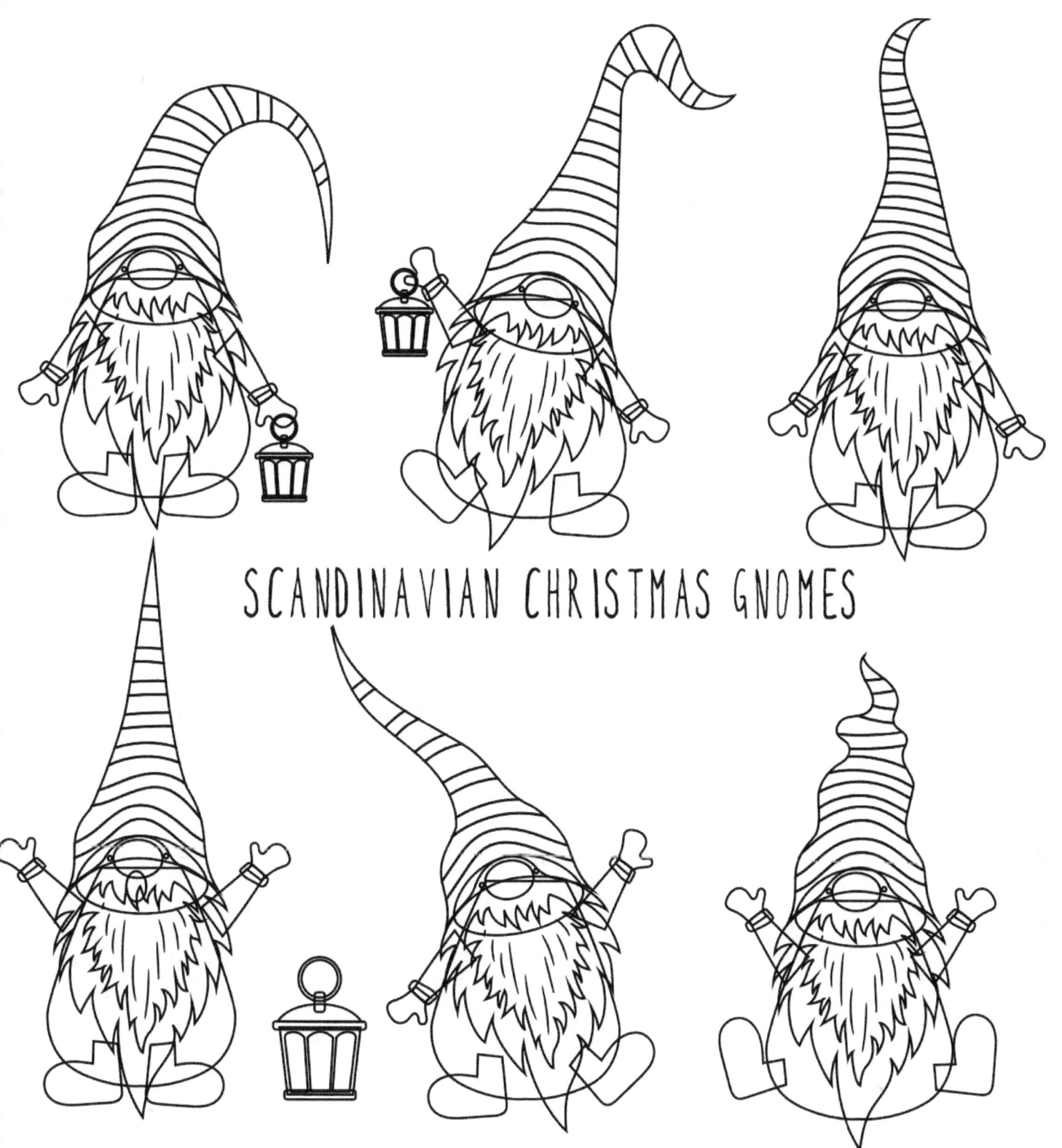

SCANDINAVIAN CHRISTMAS GNOMES

www.ingramcontent.com/pod-product-compliance
Lightning Source LLC
Chambersburg PA
CBHW081544220526
45467CB00010B/3314